G000273871

STRE

Derby

Belper, Castle Donington

First published 2007 by

Philip's, a division of
Octopus Publishing Group Ltd
2–4 Heron Quays, London E14 4JP
An Hachette Livre UK Company

First edition 2007
First impression 2007

ISBN-10 0-540-09169-3
ISBN-13 978-0-540-09169-0
© Philip's 2007

This product includes mapping data licensed
from Ordnance Survey®, with the
permission of the Controller of Her Majesty's
Stationery Office.© Crown copyright 2007.
All rights reserved.
Licence number 100011710

No part of this publication may be
reproduced, stored in a retrieval system or
transmitted in any form or by any means,
electronic, mechanical, photocopying,
recording or otherwise, without the
permission of the Publishers and the
copyright owner.

To the best of the Publishers' knowledge, the
information in this atlas was correct at the
time of going to press. No responsibility can
be accepted for any errors or their
consequences.

The representation in this atlas of a road,
track or path is no evidence of the existence
of a right of way.

Ordnance Survey and the OS symbol are
registered trademarks of Ordnance Survey,
the national mapping agency of Great Britain

Photographic acknowledgements:
VIII, IX Travel and Places / Alamy

Printed by Toppan, China

Contents

Key to map symbols

Roads

(12)	**Motorway** with junction number
A34	**Primary route** – dual, single carriageway
A40	**A road** – dual, single carriageway
B1289	**B road** – dual, single carriageway
	Through-route – dual, single carriageway
	Minor road – dual, single carriageway
	Rural track, private road or narrow road in urban area
	Path, bridleway, byway open to all traffic, road used as a public path
	Road under construction
	Pedestrianised area
	Gate or obstruction to traffic restrictions may not apply at all times or to all vehicles
P P&R	**Parking, Park and Ride**

Railways

	Railway
	Miniature railway
	Metro station, private railway station

Emergency services

◆ ◆	**Ambulance station, coastguard station**
◆ ◆	**Fire station, police station**
H ✚	**Hospital, Accident and Emergency entrance to hospital**

General features

✛ PO	**Place of worship, Post Office**
i	**Information centre** (open all year)
● ▭	**Bus or coach station, shopping centre**
	Important buildings, schools, colleges, universities and hospitals
	Woods, built-up area
Tumulus FORT	**Non-Roman antiquity, Roman antiquity**

Leisure facilities

⚐ 🚐	**Camping site, caravan site**
⚑ ✕	**Golf course, picnic site**

Boundaries

• • • • •	**Postcode boundaries**
— • —	**County and unitary authority boundaries**

Water features

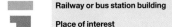

River Ouse	**Tidal water, water name**
	Non-tidal water – lake, river, canal or stream
⟨ ⏐	**Lock, weir**

Enlarged mapping only

	Railway or bus station building
	Place of interest
	Parkland

Scales

Blue pages: 4½ inches to 1 mile 1:14 080

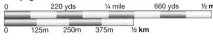

```
0        220 yds      ¼ mile       660 yds       ½ m
0     125m    250m    375m      ½ km
```

Red pages: 7 inches to 1 mile 1:9051

```
0      110 yds     220 yds    330 yds     ¼ mile
0          125m         250m        375m      ½ km
```

Adjoining page indicators The colour of the arrow and the band indicates the scale of the adjoining page (see above)

Abbreviations

Acad	Academy	Mkt	Market
Allot Gdns	Allotments	Meml	Memorial
Cemy	Cemetery	Mon	Monument
C Ctr	Civic Centre	Mus	Museum
CH	Club House	Obsy	Observatory
Coll	College	Pal	Royal Palace
Crem	Crematorium	PH	Public House
Ent	Enterprise	Recn Gd	Recreation Ground
Ex H	Exhibition Hall	Resr	Reservoir
Ind Est	Industrial Estate	Ret Pk	Retail Park
IRB Sta	Inshore Rescue Boat Station	Sch	School
		Sh Ctr	Shopping Centre
Inst	Institute	TH	Town Hall/House
Ct	Law Court	Trad Est	Trading Estate
L Ctr	Leisure Centre	Univ	University
LC	Level Crossing	Wks	Works
Liby	Library	YH	Youth Hostel

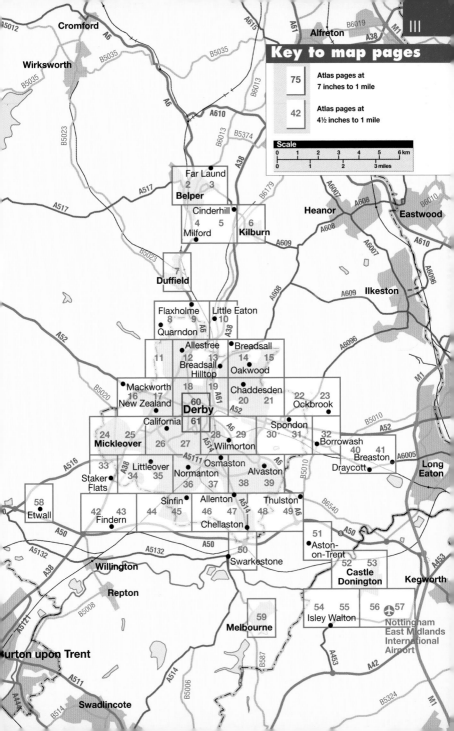

III

Cromford
Alfreton

Wirksworth

Key to map pages

| 75 | Atlas pages at 7 inches to 1 mile |
| 42 | Atlas pages at 4½ inches to 1 mile |

Scale
0 1 2 3 4 5 6 km
0 1 2 3 miles

Heanor
Eastwood

Far Laund
2 3
Belper
Cinderhill
4 5 6
Milford
Kilburn

Ilkeston

7
Duffield

Flaxholme
8 9 10
Little Eaton
Quarndon

Allestree
11 12 13
Breadsall
14 15
Breadsall
Hilltop
Oakwood

Mackworth
16 17 18 19
Chaddesden
20 21
22 23
New Zealand
Derby
60
61
Ockbrook

California
Spondon
30 31
32
24 25 26 27 28 29
Wilmorton
Borrowash
40 41
Breaston
Mickleover
Draycott
Long
Eaton

Osmaston
33 34 35
Littleover
Normanton
Alvaston
Staker
Flats
36 37 38 39

Sinfin
Allenton
Thulston
42 43 44 45 46 47 48 49
Findern
Chellaston

58
Etwall

51
Aston-
on-Trent
50
Swarkestone

Willington
52 53
Castle
Donington
Kegworth

Repton

59
Melbourne
54 55 56 57
Isley Walton
Nottingham
East Midlands
International
Airport

Burton upon Trent

Swadlincote

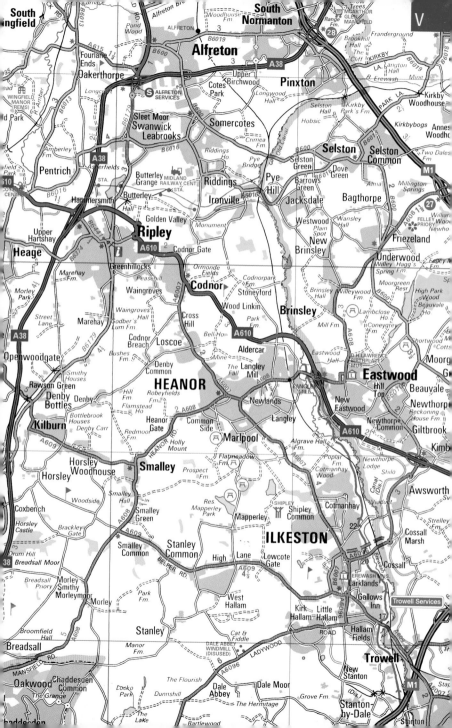

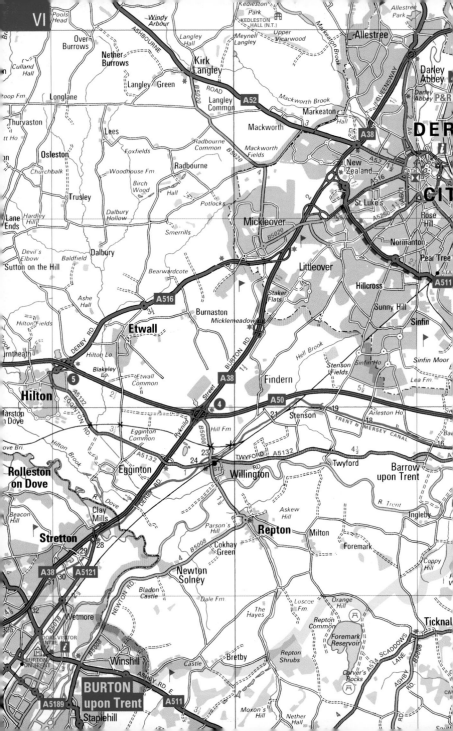

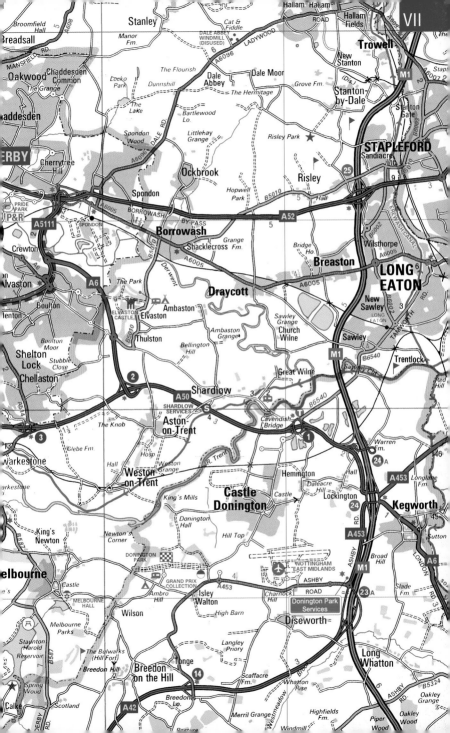

Visitor Attractions

Museums and Galleries

Derby Museum & Art Gallery *The Strand, Derby* Derby Museum and Art Gallery houses a wide range of important and attractive collections, covering porcelain, especially that produced in the area, archaeology, history, local regiments, geology and wildlife and paintings, including the largest collection of works by the 18th-century artist, Joseph Wright of Derby. The Bonnie Prince Charlie room details Derby's role in the 1745 Jacobite uprising, while local geology and wildlife are explored in the Time Tunnel walk-in cave and discovery area. ☎01332 716659 💻www.derby.gov.uk 60 B3

Donington Grand Prix Collection *Donington Park Racing Circuit, Castle Donington, Derby* The largest collection of Grand Prix racing cars in the world, including cars driven by Ayrton Senna, Stirling Moss, Nigel Mansell, Jackie Stewart, Fangio and Alain Prost, Jim Clark's Lotus 25 and the largest collection of McLarens in one place. ☎01332 811027 💻www.doningtoncollection.com 55 A2

Pickford's House Museum *41 Friar Gate, Derby* A museum of Georgian life and costume in which the dining room, drawing room and morning room, bedroom and dressing room, servant's bedroom, kitchen and laundry have been reconstructed, together with a cellar, pantry and housekeeper's cupboard, so that visitors get an idea of what life was like both above and below stairs in Georgian times. One of the cellars is equipped as an air-raid shelter of the 1940s. There is also a display of toys and a toy theatre, as well as examples of the museum's collection of historic costumes and textiles. ☎01332 255363 💻www.derby.gov.uk 18 B1

▲ *Curzon family memorial, All Saints' Church, Kedleston*

The Silk Mill *Silk Mill Lane, off Full Street, Derby* On the site of the world's oldest factory, the silk mills built by George Sorocold in 1702 and 1717, the Silk Mill Museum tells the story of the industrial heritage of Derby, including Rolls-Royce aero engines and the railway industry as well as other local industries such as mining, foundry work and pottery. It is part of the UNESCO World Heritage Site of the Derwent Valley Mills. ☎01332 255308 💻www.derby.gov.uk 60 B4

Historic Sites

The Clusters *Belper* Between Joseph Street and Long Row are the cottages built for the families of workers for the Strutts, the local mill owners, in the 19th century. Various types of houses were built for different levels of workers, with those of the supervisors being markedly bigger than the rest. 2 B2

North Mill *Bridgefoot, Belper, Derby* At the heart of the UNESCO World Heritage Site of the Derwent Valley Mills, which runs from the Silk Mill in Derby to Matlock Bath and includes Arkwright's mill at Cromford, this cotton mill, erected in 1804, is a forerunner of skyscrapers and is one of the oldest industrial water-powered cotton-spinning mills to survive. An early example of an iron-framed 'fire-proof' building, it had both a hot air heating system and air extraction to remove the cotton dust. The top floor of the factory housed a school where the mill-workers' children were taught on Sundays. The Derwent Valley Visitor Centre has a museum about the textile industry and the industrial revolution. 💻www.belpernorthmill.org.uk ☎01773 880474 2 B3

Places of Worship

All Saints Cathedral *Iron Gate, Derby* Originally founded as a collegiate church in 943AD, but the earliest part of the building still standing is the Tudor tower, built between 1510 and 1530. In 1549, it became the parish church and all the college buildings were destroyed. In the 18th century, all but the tower was demolished, and a new church built around it by James Gibbs. In 1927, it became the cathedral for the new diocese of Derby and in the 1960s an eastern extension and several new stained glass windows were added. ☎01332 345848 💻www.derbycathedral.org 60 B3/4

St Michael with St Mary *Church Square, Melbourne* Begun in about 1120, Melbourne's parish church is often described as one of the most beautiful churches in England. Except for the east end, much of the Norman stonework remains, despite Victorian restoration. The crossing arch has unusual carved capitals and a fragment of wall painting. 💻www.melbourneparishchurch.co.uk 59 B2

Other Sights

Calke Abbey & Park (NT) *nr Ticknall, 10 miles S of Derby, off the A514* A great Baroque country house in decline, with extraordinary contents from the 18th and 19th centuries, an historic park and restored garden. The house is full of invisible corridors and underground tunnels, and the grounds include a secret garden, walled kitchen and cutting gardens, ice house, gardener's bothy and orangery with peach house, set within a 600-acre National Nature Reserve. ☎01332 863 822 💻www.nationaltrust.org.uk

Kedleston Hall (NT) *Kedleston Road, northwest of Derby, off the A38* A masterpiece of neo-classical architecture built for the Curzon family between 1759 and 1765, with luxurious Adam interiors, landscaped gardens with stunning displays of azaleas and rhododendrons in early summer and open parkland with cascades and lakes. The Eastern Museum has the collections of Lord Curzon, Viceroy of India. All Saints' Church (not NT) contains memorials and monuments of the Curzon family. ☎01332 842191 💻www.nationaltrust.org.uk

Royal Crown Derby *194 Osmaston Road, Derby* Visitor centre, museum and tours around the world-famous bone-china factory. The company first started producing high-quality porcelain in the 1750s, and moved here in the 1870s. The museum has a comprehensive collection of pieces from more than 250 years of production, including very early figures by Andre Planche, one of the founders of the company, the Imari patterns for which the factory is renowned, eggshell china and examples of the china commissioned for the Titanic. There is also a complete collection of Royal Crown Derby paperweights. ☎01332 712800 💻www.royal-crown-derby.co.uk 61 C1

Green Spaces

Allestree Park *Duffield Road, Allestree, Derby* With more than 320 acres of parkland and woodland, Allestree Park also offers plenty of wildlife, an 18-hole golf course, an angling lake, an orienteering course, a pet's corner and a field of Jacob sheep. The circular walk takes about three hours. ☎01332 715507 💻www.derby.gov.uk 8 C1

Alvaston Park *off London Road, Derby* Established in 1913, Alvaston has cycling, a children's playground, BMX track and skate half pipe, cricket and football pitches, tennis and basketball courts, walks, a fishing lake and a nature reserve. ☎01332 715507 💻www.derby.gov.uk 29 B2

Arboretum Park *Reginald Street, Normanton, Derby* England's first public park, the Arboretum was given to the town by a local mill owner, Joseph Strutt, as a place for local people to exercise and relax. There is a play area, bowling green, tennis courts, cricket nets and a ball court, as well as a tree trail. ☎01332 292612. 💻www.derby.gov.uk 28 A2

Darley Park *Darley Park Drive, Derby* A large park, conveniently close to the city centre, Darley Park has wide open spaces and unspoiled parkland to wander through and is home to several sports clubs. It also houses the National Collection of Viburnum and Hydrangea and has a tree trail.
☎ 01332 715507 🖳 www.darley.gov.uk 12 C1

Elvaston Castle Country Park *Borrowash Road, east of Derby, off the B5010* More than 200 acres of woodland, parkland and formal gardens. As well as its many waymarked walks and bridleways, it has an Old English Garden, a riding centre, children's play area, a nature trail and a local nature reserve.
☎ 01332 571342 🖳 www.derbyshire.gov.uk

Markeaton Park *Ashbourne Road, Derby* One of the most popular attractions in Derby, especially for children, this park has vast areas of open parkland and the Mundy Play Centre, and also offers a golf course, pitch and putt, a boating lake, canoeing, fishing, a children's lake and paddling pool, karting, crazy golf, a miniature railway and a craft village. 🖳 www.derby.gov.uk
☎ 01332 715507 17 B3

Melbourne Hall Gardens *Melbourne Hall, Church Square, Melbourne, Derbyshire* Colourful and tranquil 18th-century landscape gardens originally designed by Thomas Coke, with paths, streams, statues and garden buildings. (Hall open in August only.)
☎ 01332 862 502 🖳 www.melbournehall.com 59 C2

River Gardens *Matlock Road, Belper, Derbyshire* Beautiful gardens with stunning views over the Derwent Valley, developed from the osier beds used by the nearby cotton mills. Rowing boats for hire and children's play area. Regular concerts and theatre performances in summer. ☎ 01773 841488
🖳 www.ambervalley.gov.uk 2 B3

Activities

Assembly Rooms *Market Place, Derby* Derby's leading entertainment venue, the Assembly Rooms has a year-round programme including an orchestral season, comedy, rock and pop events and family entertainment 🖳 www.assemblyrooms-derby.co.uk
☎ 01332 255800 60 B3

The Asterdale Club *Borrowash Road (opp Borrowash Rd), Spondon, Derby* Home to Derby City RLFC. 🖳 www.derbycityrlfc.co.uk
☎ 01332 668656 31 B3

The County Ground *Grandstand Road, Derby* Home of Derbyshire CCC. ☎ 01332 383211
🖳 www.derbyshireccc.com 19 B2

Derby Dance Centre *Chapel Street, Derby* The only dedicated dance house in the East Midlands with a 134-seat studio theatre and two dance studios. Stages a wide range of modern dance productions.
☎ 01332 370 911 🖳 www.derbydance.co.uk 60 B4

Derby Playhouse *Westfield Derby (Eagle Centre), Theatre Walk, Derby* Hosts a wide

▲ *Silk Mill Museum*

range of productions from Shakespeare to new commissions. 🖳 www.derbyplayhouse.co.uk ☎ 01332 363275 61 C2

Donington Park Motor Racing Circuit *Castle Donington, Derby* As well as major events such as rounds of the Moto GP and Superbike Championship, the circuit holds track days and offers opportunities to learn to drive supercars. 🖳 www.donington-park.co.uk
☎ 01332 810 048 54 C3

Guildhall Theatre *Market Place, Derby* This theatre provides a blend of professional touring theatre and music events, as well as offering a venue for many amateur productions. 🖳 www.assemblyrooms-derby.co.uk
☎ 01332 255800 60 B3

Lancaster Sports Centre *Chapel St, Derby* This centre's facilities include a gym, women-only gym, sports hall and activity rooms, while activities on offer include badminton, basketball, five-a-side football, gymnastics, hockey, martial arts, netball, short tennis and trampolining. 🖳 www.derby.gov.uk ☎ 01332 361549 60 B4

The Market Hall *Market Place, Derby* A Victorian covered market divided into four distinct areas, with 140 stalls and shops: Balcony, Poultry Market, Fish Market/Lock-up Yard and the Market Hall Shops. Also has cafés and a flea market. Monday to Saturday.
☎ 01332 255573 60 B3

Moorways Sports Centre *Moor Lane, Allenton, Derby* One of the largest sports facilities in the Midlands, Moorways offers a gym, work-out studio, indoor cycling, swimming pools, badminton and squash courts, athletics track, synthetic and grass pitches and a wide variety of fitness activities. ☎ 01332 363686
🖳 www.derby.gov.uk 37 C2

Odeon Cinema *Meteor Centre, Mansfield Road, Derby* 🖳 www.odeon.co.uk ☎ 0871 2244007 60 B4

Pride Park Stadium *off Royal Way, Derby* Home of Derby County FC. ☎ 0870 444 1884 🖳 www.dcfc.premiumtv.co.uk 29 A3

Queen's Leisure Centre *Cathedral Road, Derby* Facilities include a gym, workout studio, squash courts and three swimming pools, with workout classes, racketball and aqua-fit and aqua-natal classes. ☎ 01332 716 620 🖳 www.derby.gov.uk 60 B4

Showcase Cinema *Foresters Park Centre, Osmaston Park Rd / Sinfin Lane, Derby* 🖳 www.showcasecinemas.co.uk ☎ 0871 220 1000 36 C3

Westfield Derby (Eagle Centre) *Albion Street, Derby* More than 150 stores and places to eat, as well as the largest indoor market in Britain. The extension is due for completion in 2008, including the new 12-screen Cinema-de-Lux. 🖳 www.westfield.com ☎ 01332 366383 61 C2

Information

🅸 **Derby Tourist Information Centre** *Assembly Rooms, Market Place, Derby* ☎ 01332 255802 🖳 www.visitderby.co.uk 60 B3

Derby City Council *The Council House, Corporation Street, Derby* ☎ 01332 293111 🖳 www.derby.gov.uk

East Midlands Airport *Castle Donington, Derby* 🖳 www.eastmidlandsairport.com ☎ 0871 919 9000 57 A3

NCP Car Parking ☎ 0670 606 7050 🖳 www.ncp.co.uk

National Rail Enquiries ☎ 08457 484950 🖳 www.nationalrail.co.uk

Public Transport ☎ 01332 715045 🖳 www.derby.gov.uk

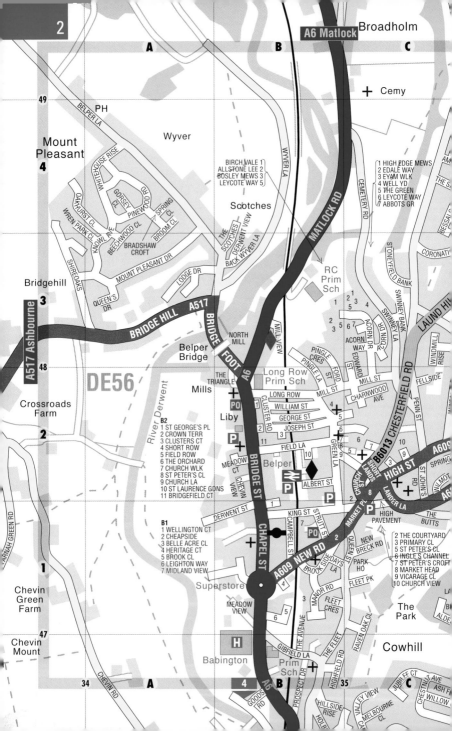

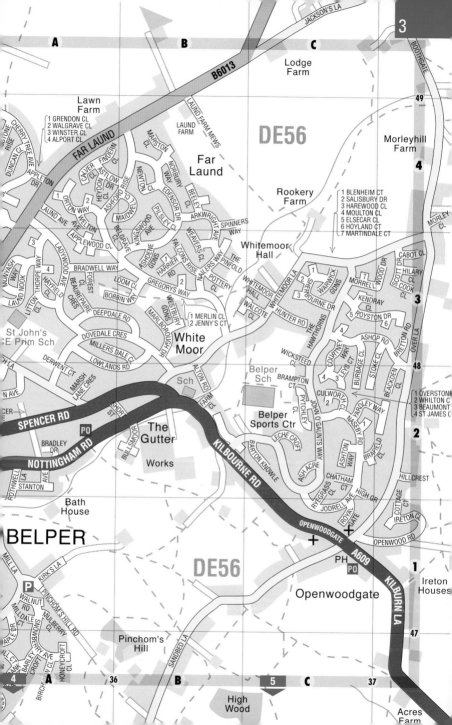

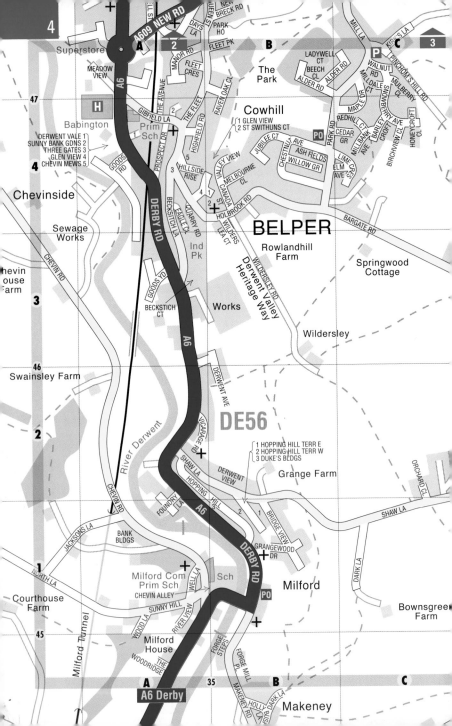

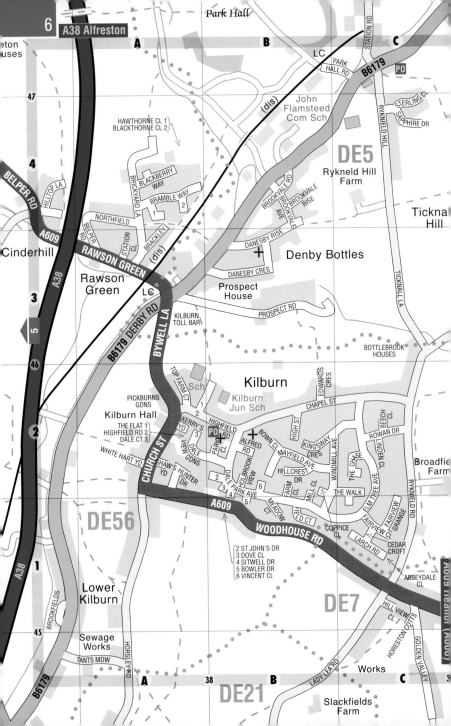

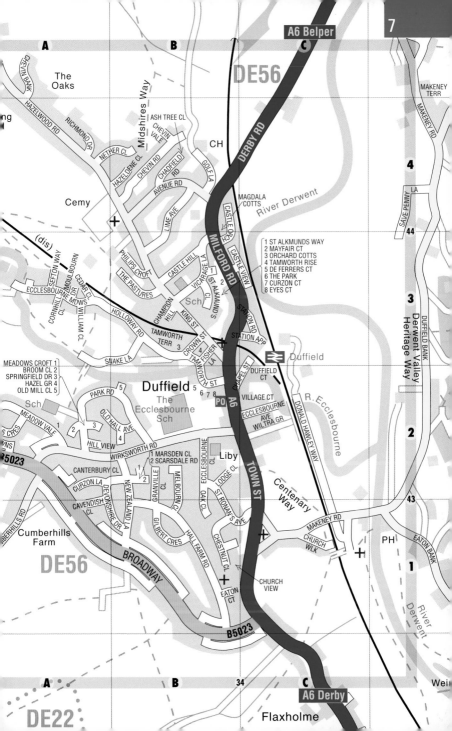

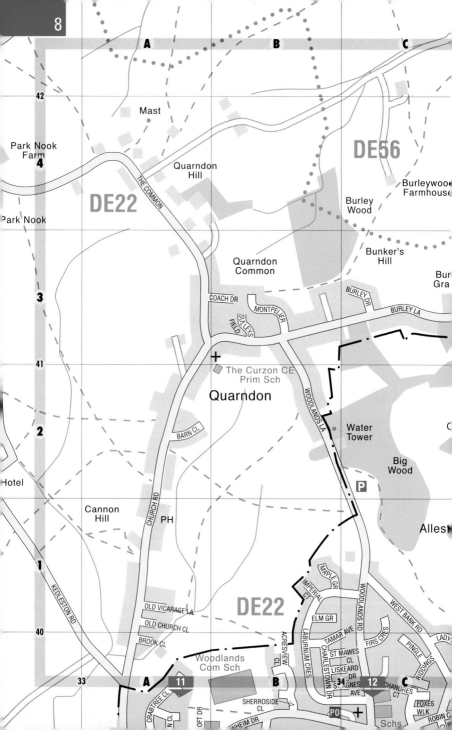

A   B   C

42

Mast

Park Nook
Farm

4

DE56

Quarndon
Hill

Park Nook

DE22

THE COMMON

Burleywoo
Farmhouse

Burley
Wood

Quarndon
Common

Bunker's
Hill

Bur
Gra

3

COACH DR

BURLEY DR

BURLEY LA

MONTPELIER

SULLEYS FIELD

41

The Curzon CE
Prim Sch

WOODLANDS LA

Quarndon

Water
Tower

C

2

BARN CL

Big
Wood

Hotel

Cannon
Hill

CHURCH RD

PH

P

Allest

1

KEDLESTON RD

MAPLE GR

IMPERIAL CT

WOODLANDS RD

WEST BANK RD

DE22

LADY

ELM GR

TAMAR AVE

FIRS CRES

PINGLE

RIDDINGS

OLD VICARAGE LA

CL

CHARLESTOWN DR

40

OLD CHURCH CL

ACRESVIEW CL

LABURNUM CRES

ST MAWES
CL

DR

CHANDRES
CT

BROOK CL

LISKEARD

ST AGNES
AVE

FOXES
WLK

33   A   11   B   34   12   C

ROBIN CL

Woodlands
Com Sch

SHERROSIDE
CL

PO

ROBIN

N CL

FT DR

HEIM DR

Schs

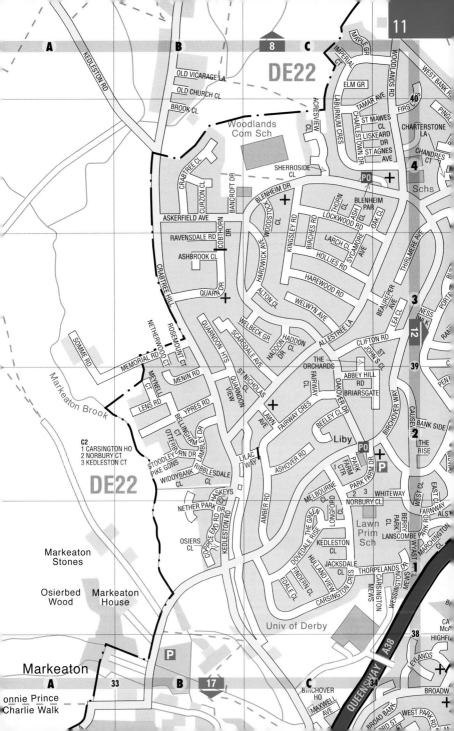

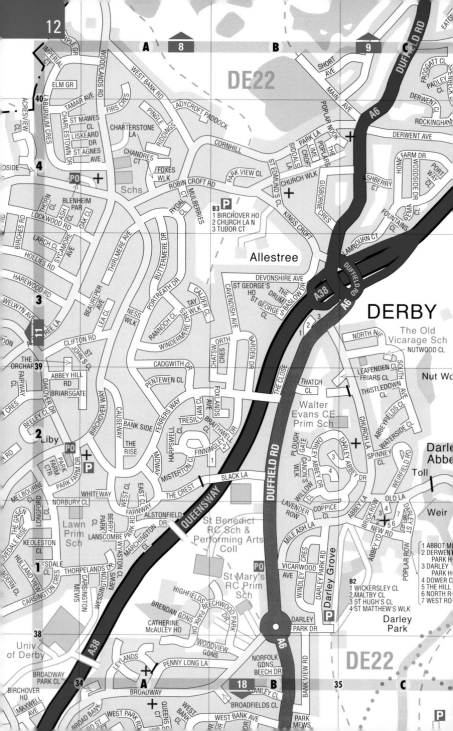

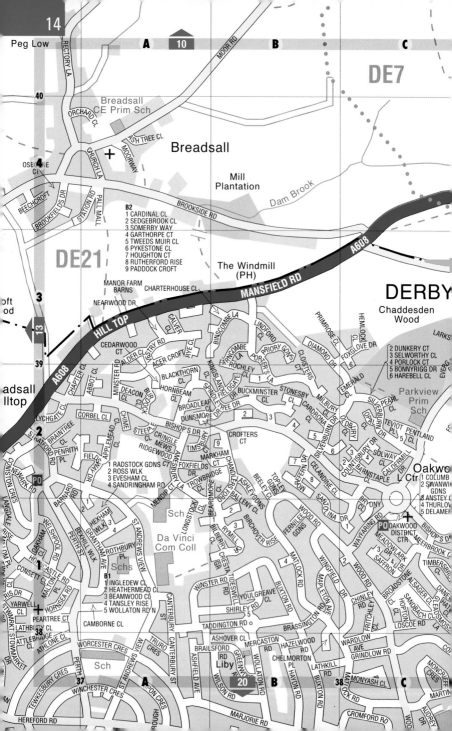

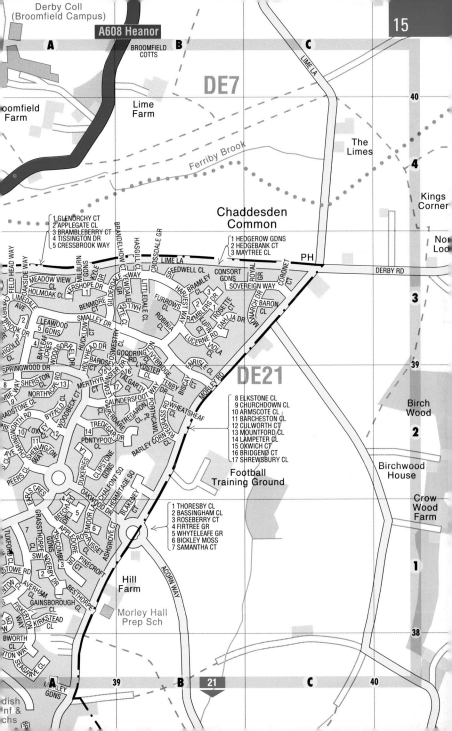

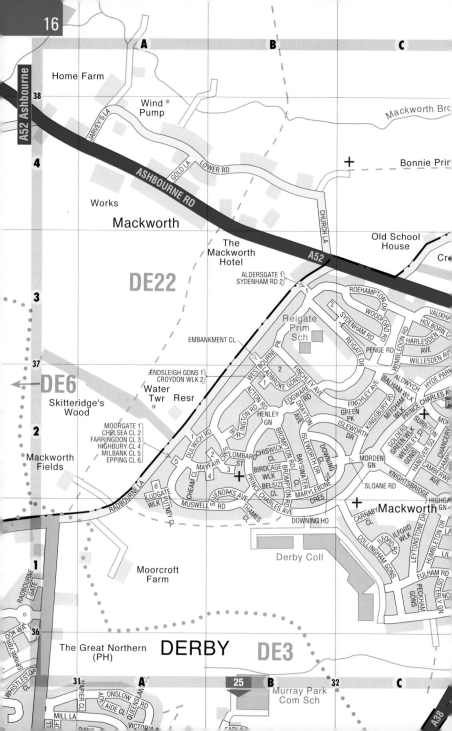

A B C

Home Farm

Wind Pump

A52 Ashbourne

38

4

JARVEY'S LA

GOLD LA

LOWER RD

ASHBOURNE RD

Mackworth Bro

Works

Mackworth

A52

CHURCH LA

Bonnie Prin

Old School House

Cr

The Mackworth Hotel

DE22

ALDERSGATE 1
SYDENHAM RD 2

ROEHAMPTON DR

WOODFORD RD

VAUXH

HOLBORN LN

Reigate Prim Sch

SYDENHAM RD

WIMBLEDON RD

HARLESDEN AVE

EMBANKMENT CL

PENGE RD

REIGATE DR

WILLESDEN AVE

3

ENDSLEIGH GDNS 1
CROYDON WLK 2

WESTBOURNE PK

ADBROKE GDNS

FINCHLEY AVE

ALDWYCH

HYDE PARK

37

DE6

Water Twr Resr

ACTON RD

EDGWARE RD

DRAYTON AVE

FINCHLEY GREEN PK

KINGSBURY RD

ISLEWORTH DR

BALHAM WLK

MITCHAM WLK

PRINCE CHARLES A

SURBITON

Skitteridge's Wood

BLR

ISLINGTON RD

HENLEY GN

BROMPTON RD

BAYSWATER

ISLEWORTH DR

DOWNING RD

GOLDERS GREEN WLK

WEMBLEY GDNS

HANOVER SQ

CAMBERWE

CHANCER

MOORGATE 1
CHELSEA CL 2
FARRINGDON CL 3
HIGHBURY CL 4
MILBANK CL 5
EPPING CL 6

DULWICH RD

LOMBARD ST

CHISWICK CL

BIRDCAGE WLK

BROMPTON RD

BELSIZE CL

MORDEN GN

KNIGHTSBRIDGE

SLOANE RD

2

Mackworth Fields

MAYFAIR CL

CHEAM CL

MARYLEBONE CRES

HIGHGA

Mackworth GN

RADBOURNE LA

LUDGATE WLK

PUTNEY CL

MUSWELL

SEVENOAKS RD

PRINCE CHARLES AVE

THAMES CL

DOWNING HO

CARNABY CL

COLLINGHAM GDNS

ILFORD RD

ILFORD WLK

LEYTONSTONE DR

HUMBLETON DR

LIL

Derby Coll

1

RADBOURNE GATE

Moorcroft Farm

FULHAM RD

PECKHAM GDNS

OSTERL

WHISTLESTOP CL

OOK WAY

SPINNEYBR

36

The Great Northern (PH)

DERBY DE3

A38

31

NAPIER CL

ONSLOW RD

ADELAIDE CL

QUEENSLAN

A

25

B

Murray Park Com Sch

32

C

MILL LA

VICTORIA

EARL

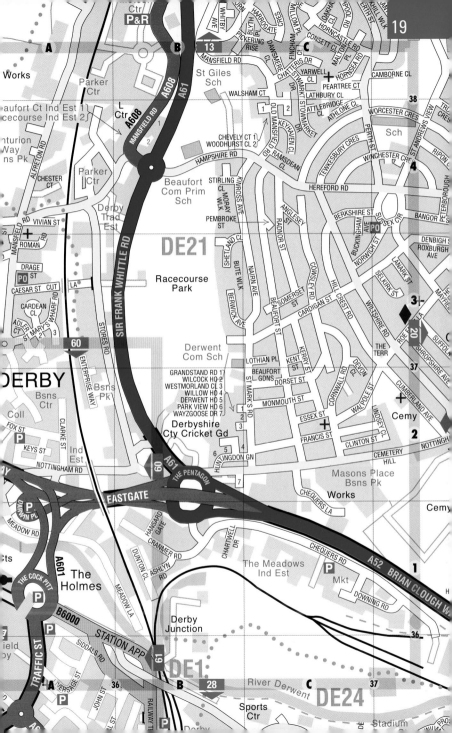

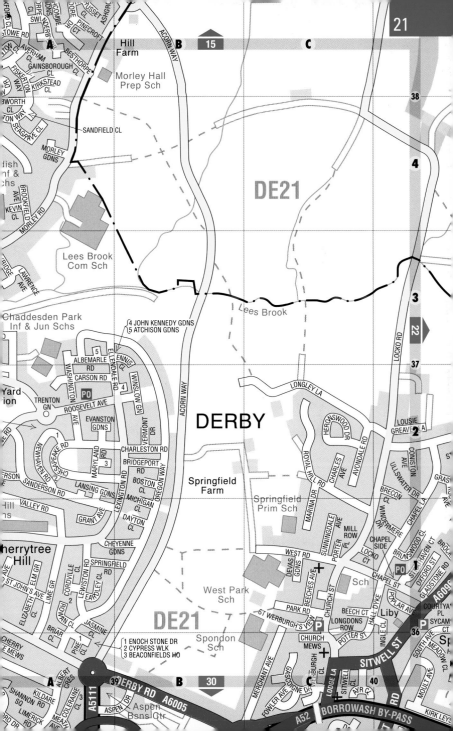

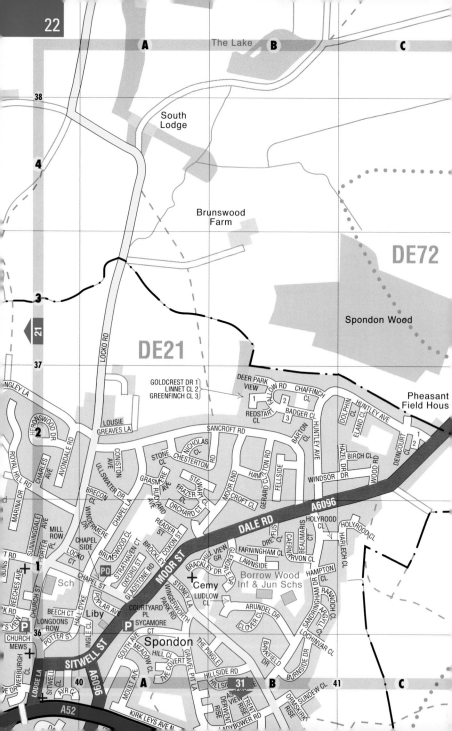

A   B   C

36
Silverhill
Wood

4

DE6

Potlocks
Farm

Hackwood
Farm

STARFLOWER WAY
ZOOK WA
CRYSTAL CL
BROOK RD
WHISTLESTOP
RADBOURNE GATE
B5020
Th

CUTLER WAY 1
LANTERN GR 2
MEWS CT 3

FARBOURNE DR
WHISTLESTOP CL 3

MILL
MILL CROFT
MICKLERO

INGLEWOOD AVE
BROMLEY CL
STAVERTON DR
WELLAND CL
BELVEDERE CL
TIVERTON CL
CAMELLIA CL
LANGFORD RD
HAILSHAM CL
WESTHALL CL
BROOMHILL CL
MICKLERC

STATION RD

MILL

3

Bonnie Prince Charlie Walk

SAXONDALE AVE
ROYDON CL
OLTON RD
STANSTEAD RD
RIGSBY CL
ASHTON CL
UPCHURCH CL
LOXTON CL
MARFLEET
CHILSON DR
ROTHWELL RD
CHESTNUT A
ROYDON RD

SANDOWN AVE
MILTON CL
BARWELL CL
SHELFORD
BRAMPTON CL
DAVENTRY CL
KINGSMUIR RD
CHELMSFORD CT
STARCROSS
SILVERHILL PRIM SCH
MALVERN CL
WINDSOR CT
MOORLA

Silverhill
Prim Sch

HOYLAKE DR
DRYSDALE RD
DENVER CL
APPLETR
WLK

SOUTHGATE
NASEBY CL
WIGMORE CL
SWAYFIELD
DRAYCOTT DR
SEATON CL
HOYLAKE CT
EDALE
AVE
M

Bean Hole
Plantation

ADWICK CL
TAPLOW CL
BARNWOOD CL
STAINES CL
CHERTSEY RD
WHENBY CL
WEST DR
FARNWORTH RD
FENTON RD

Hack
ood

35

Osierbed
Wood

2

DE3

DRESDEN CL
LAMBROOK CL
GREENSIDE CT
LADYBANK RD
GLENFIELD CRES
COOKHAM CL
BURNHAM DR
FARNHAM CL

HOPE AVE

Mickleover
Prim Sch

Liby

PORTLAN

THE
DOVEDALES
PARK RD

Recn
Gd

VICARAGE RD
VICARAGE CT
HILTON CL
B5020
BURLINGTON

LODGE WAY
HARTING

1

Brown Cross
Plantation

C1
1 MORLEY HO
2 BRAMBLE MEWS
3 LIMES CT
4 THE PARADE
5 MEADOW CT
6 ALL SAINTS CT

PARKSTONE CT
WEAVERS GREEN
BRUNTON CL
HOLLY CL
WARNER ST
LIDGATE CL
WENDOVER CRES
CROMER
CATTERICK DR
CHANTRY CL
PRESCOT CL
ALVERTON CL
SEDGEFIELD GREEN
CUMBRIA WLK
MICKLEOVER MANOR
UFFA MAGNA
HEDINGHAM WAY
FETWALL RD
THE ORCHARD ST
THE SQUARE
THE GREEN
IVY CT
PO
LIMES AVE
MADELEY CT
KIPLIN
ST

Bonehill
Farm

34

PAYTON CL
HOWDEN CL

WELNEY CL
THORNDON CL
INGHAM DR
THE HOLLOW
S

Hotel

A516   30   33   B   C   A51

WOODCOCK SQ
WILSON
HEDINGHAM WAY
THE

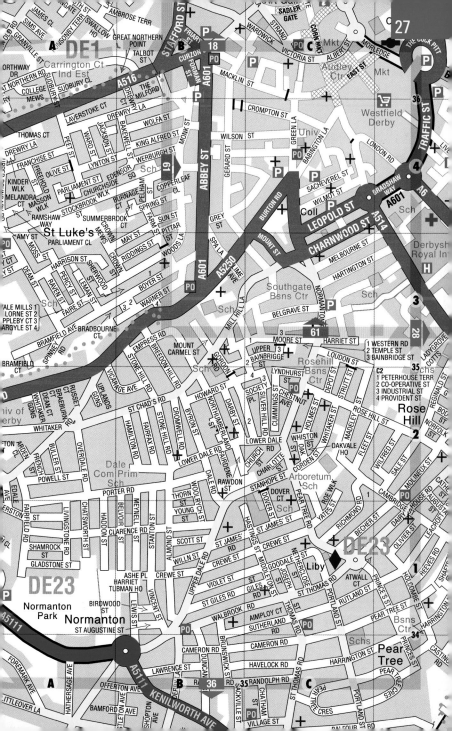

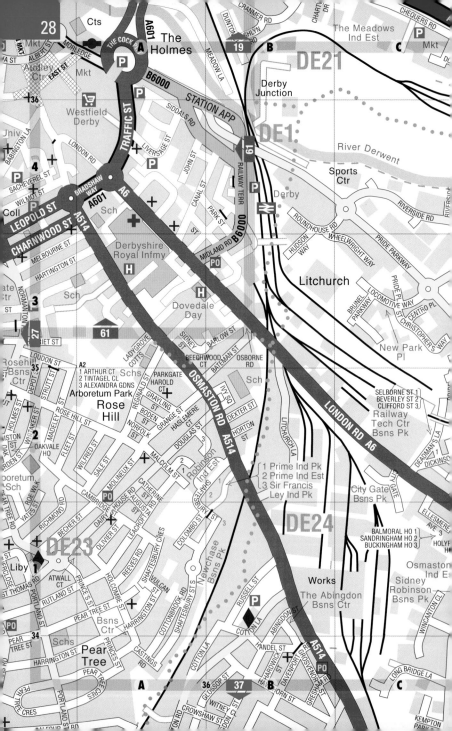

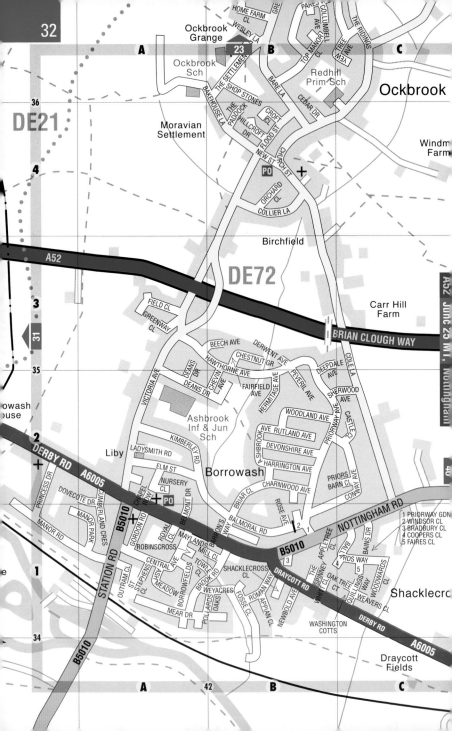

Brown Cross
Plantation

A51b Hilton, Uttoxeter

A **B** 33

PRESCOT
LIDGA
CATTERICK DR
CROMER
CHANTRY CL
WARNER ST
B5020

ALVERTON CL
SEDGEFIELD
STRETTON CL

PAXTON CL
CUMBRIA WLK
24
MICKLEOVER MANOR
UFFA MAGNA
C PO
KIPLING DR
ACACIA AVE
FREESIA DR
KESWATH CRES
SKIDAW
BOW SPK

HOWDEN CL
ETWALL RD
ORCHARD ST
THE SQUARE
LIMES AVE
MADELEY CT
MELBREAK CL
WANSFELL CL
SKIDDAW DR
LATRIG

THE GREEN
THE HOLLOW
BARF CL
LATRIG
34

Hotel
THORNDON CL
WELNEY CT
INGHAM DR
Sch
BLENCATHRA DR

4
3
2
1
HEDINGHAM WAY
BRIERFIELD WAY
GABLE
CT
4

WOODCOCK SQ
WILSON
ROUGHTON CL 1
ARDLEIGH CL 2
WRETHAM CL 3
MICKLEOVER HO 4
A516

The Grange
FINCH CRES
MALLARD WLK
THE HOLLOW
MALCOLM GR
ALLAN AVE
RONALD CL

HOSPITAL LA
LINNET HILL
MAYP

EDMUNDS SQ
KISHER CL
MERLIN WAY
LATIM CL

PLOVER CT
KING'S CL
HAVEN BAULK
JEMISON
3

REL
WREN WAY
MERLIN WAY
WATERGO LA
OXENHOPE
PEN

DUESBURY CT
SANDERLING HEATH
DE3
Staker Flats
DE23
34

DUESBURY PL
STAKER LA
A38
33

SANDPIPER LA
N HILL
2
BURGHLEY WAY

RYKNEAD WAY

Micklemeadow

Hotel
1

New Buildings
Farm
32

DE65

FINDERN LA
A 30 42 **B** 31
C 43 31
Nursery

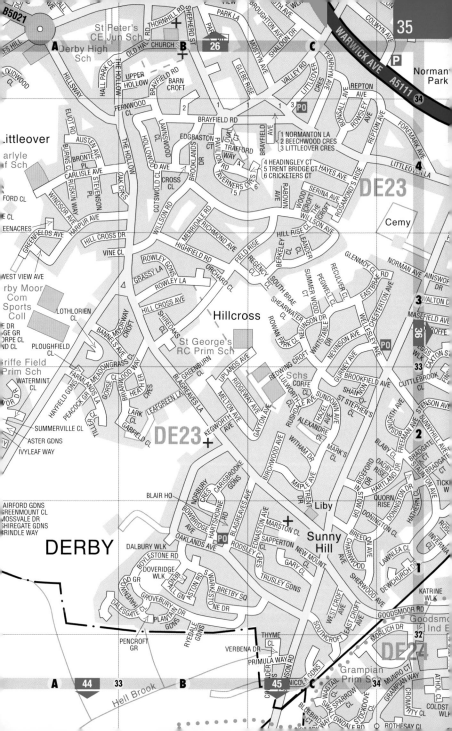

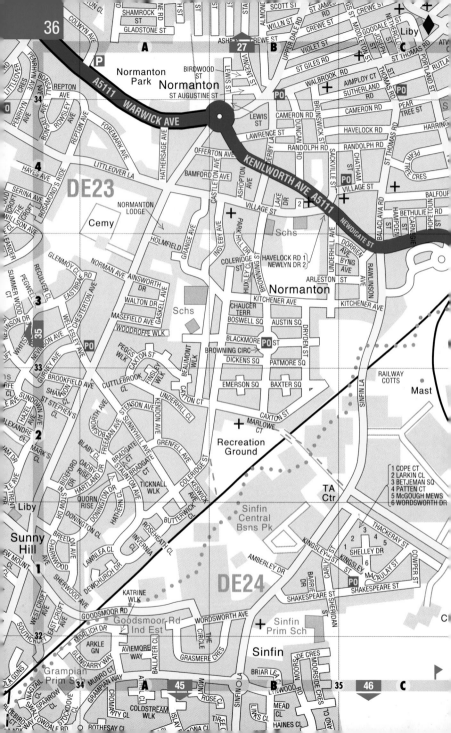

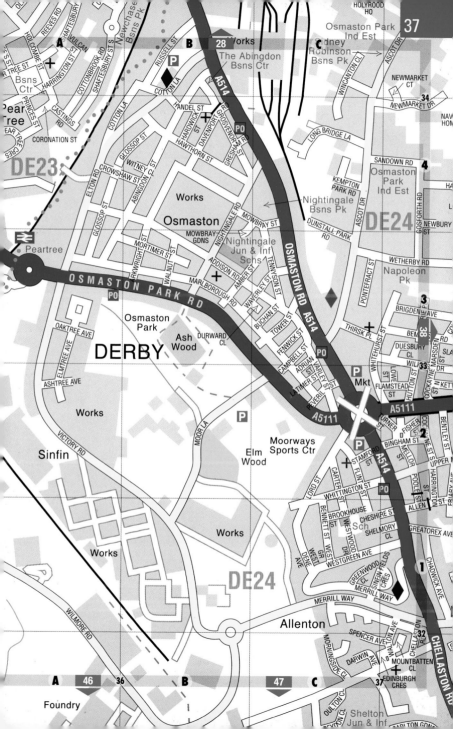

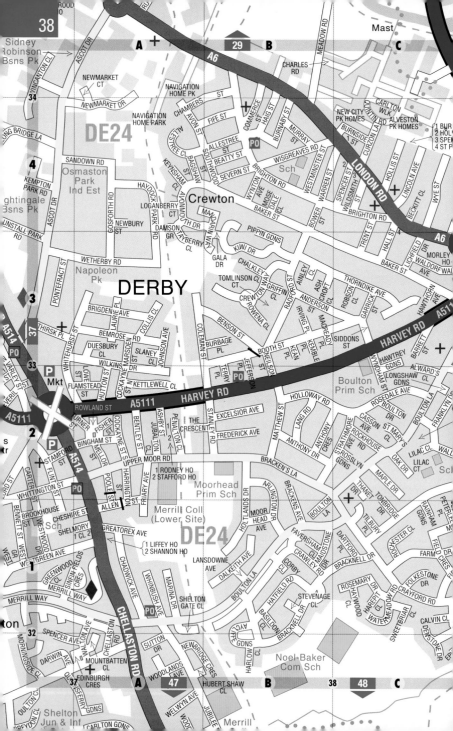

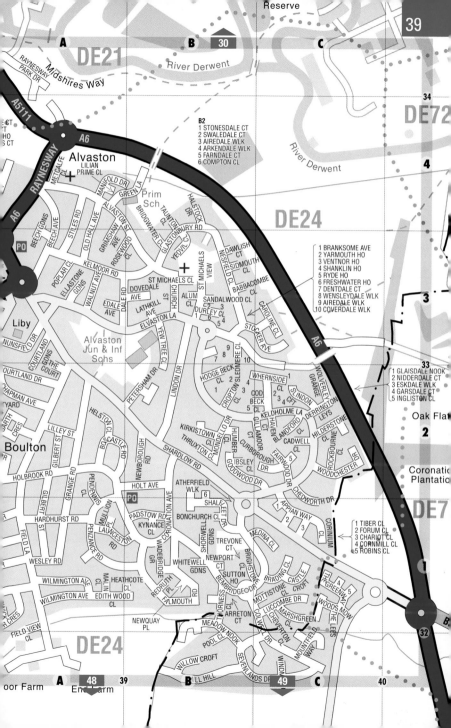

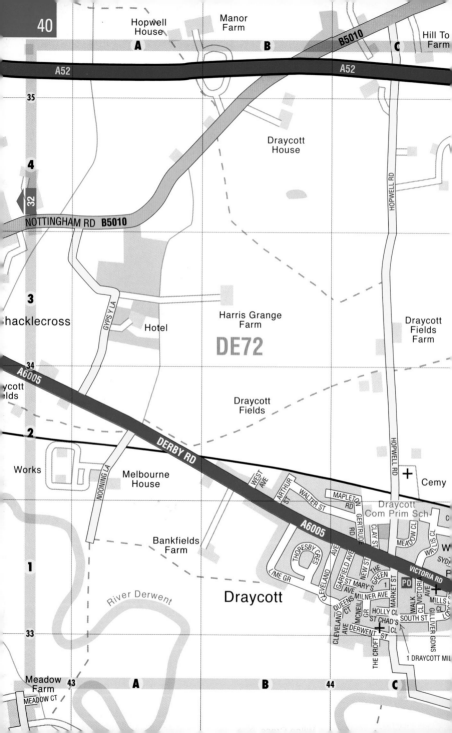

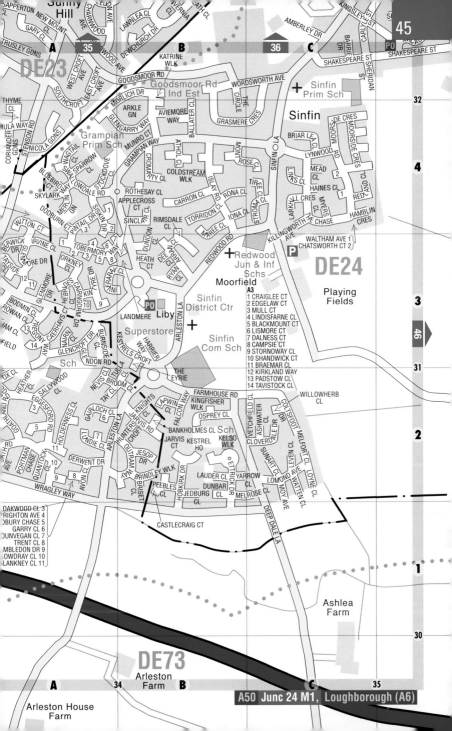

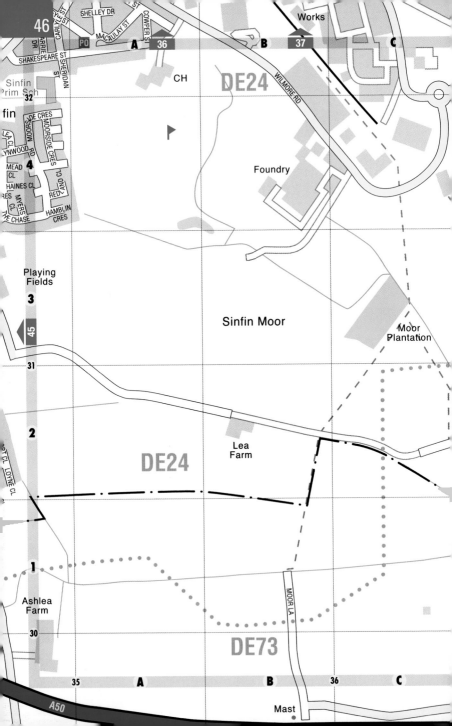

SHELLEY DR

COWPER ST

MACAULAY ST

CARLYLE ST

CARRIE DR

SHERIDAN ST

SHAKESPEARE ST

PO

A 36

Works

B 37

C

DE24

WILMORE RD

CH

Sinfin
Prim Sch
32

fin

DE CRES

LEA

BROOM

MOORSIDE CRES

LYNWOOD RD

MEAD CL

HAINES CL

AND CL

RED

4

MYERS CL

THE CHASE

HAMBLIN CRES

RES

Foundry

Playing
Fields

3

45

31

Sinfin Moor

Moor
Plantation

2

Lea
Farm

DE24

OT CL

LOYNE CL

1

Ashlea
Farm

Moor La

30

DE73

35

A

B 36

C

A50

Mast

A 38

B 39 HEATHCOTE **C**

WILMINGTON AVE EDITH WOOD CL

NEWQUAY PL

RESEMARY DR HAYWOOD CL WATERBRIAR SWEETBRIAR CALVIN CL CRAYFORD RD

BRACKNELL DR FOLKES ... FIELD CRES FIELD DR FARM CRES WESLEY RD

HATFIELD RD STEVENAGE CL BASILDON BR 32 HAREPIT DERSTONE DR EPWORTH CRES BERWICK CL BORDER CRES FIELD VIEW CL

Noel-Baker Com Sch

4

DE24

Moor Farm   End Farm

Boulton Moor

Shelton Lock

WOODMINTON DR STOURPORT DR SUTTON AVE FERNHILL BEWDLEY BAVERSTOCK SOUTH DR AVE

3 HILLSWAY EDGE HILL 47 SUTTON AVE BUTTONOAK DR BROMYARD DR CHELMARSH CL

DE73

CHEKBROOK DR

31 ASHLEIGH DR ASTORVILLE VICARAGE RD PARK RD SIMCOE LEYS MAPLE DR BLISTHIELEY LANGSETT DR LINACRES DR GRAHAM CL BACK LA WHITEHAVEN GR LINDALE WAY LEYS FIELD GDNS PINGREAVES DR THUROW WAY ACREFIELD WAY TUPHA

Stubble Close

2 SIMCOE LEYS NEWBOLD BIRCHFIELD CL LOCKINGTON CL DISEWORTH CL LITTLE MEADOW RD SANDYHILL DR CROWNLAND DR FOXDELL CHASE CL LOWS CT PINGLEHILL WAY

Fox Covert Farm

1 SILVERDALE CL
2 WARRENDALE CT
3 LEVERET CL
4 BRADMOOR GR
5 NEWGATE CL
6 HAWKSDALE CL

A514 DERBY RD ORCHARD WAY MAPLE DR REDMIRES DR SCHOOL LA WIMBOURNE CL TOWNSEND DR SLADE LANDS NETHERSIDE DR SNELSMOOR LA

Chellaston Covert

1 PO CHELLASTON PARK CT MANOR RD HIGH ST PIT CLOSE LA HIGH BARLEY HIGH ST CHURCH CL YEWS CL ST PETER'S CL GREEN AVE BENSLEY CL WILLOWBROOK GRANGE NOTHILLS CL ASTON LA

Chellaston

1 GLENWOOD RD
2 TUDOR FIELD CL
3 WOODGATE DR
4 HILL NOOK CL
5 PARKLANDS DR

30 MEADOW WAY BRIDLE CL GLENWOOD RD 3 5 4 1 2

Chellaston Sch

BOYD GR FILBERT WLK SECOND AVE MOYNE GDNS WALNUT CL WOODLANDS LA RIDGEWAY

Works

Woodlands Farm

38 **A** **50** **B** 39 **C**

REGAL GATE

49

DE72

B5010

A B C

39

ADING CL
STONE
CL CASTLE
CL CROFT
COMBE DR
MARSHGREEN
CL
CHELLERTON
CL
WINDMILL CL

A THE GREENWAY
WOODS
THE LEES
MOUNTFIELD
WAY

1 ORCHARD CL
2 THE PADDOCK

DE24

A6

B5010

BROOK
CT

HANSLYNN
OAK RD
BOBB
GROVE CL
THE PINFOLD
PH

GROVE
CT
STURGES LA
GROVE CL
YEW TREE
LA

BROAD LA

Thulston

32
Grange
Farm

OAK RD

B5010

4

Grove
Farm

Thulston Fields
Farm

B5010

3

DERBY RD

Mast

31

DE72

2

A6

A50

51

Marsh Flatts

DE73

A50

1

LLASTON LA

A50

Aston Hill

30

Aston Hill
Farm

A Uttoxeter 40 **B** CHELLASTON LA **C** 41

Knob Farm

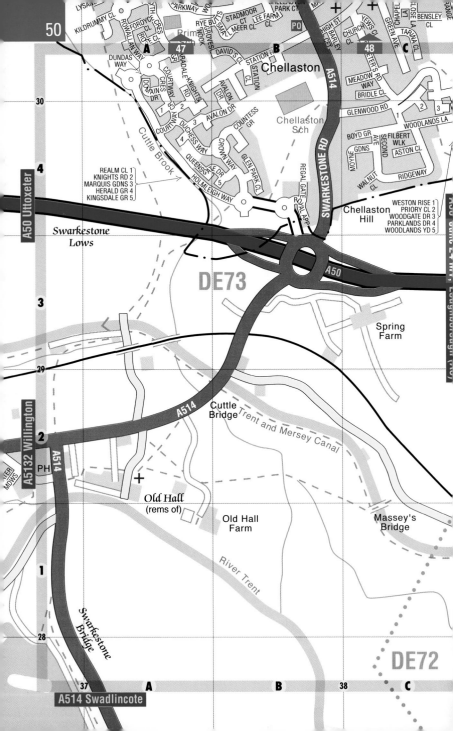

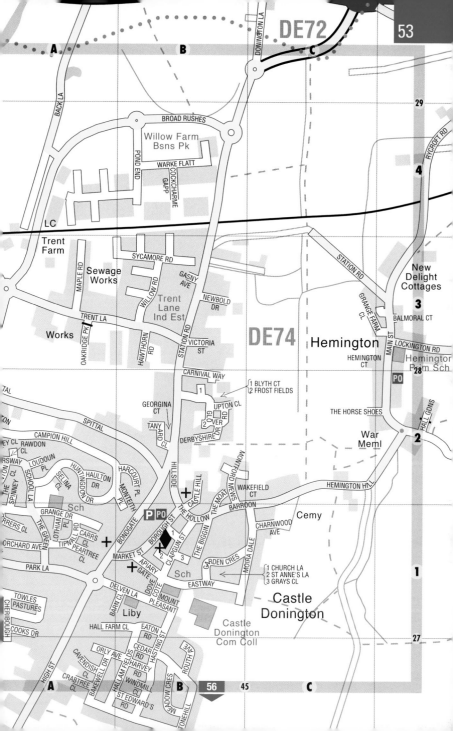

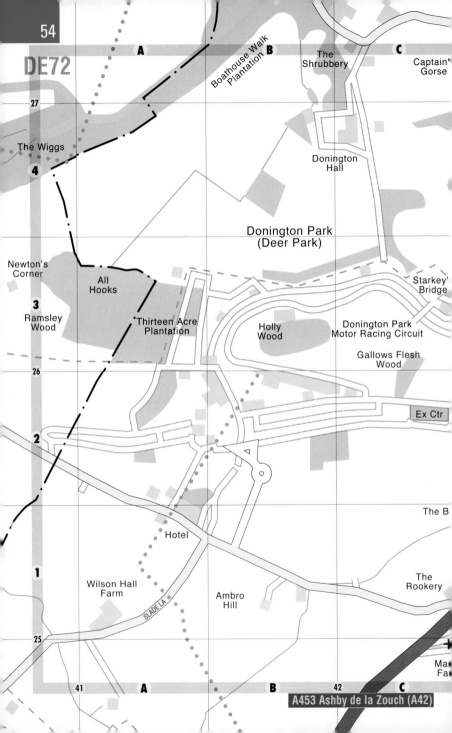

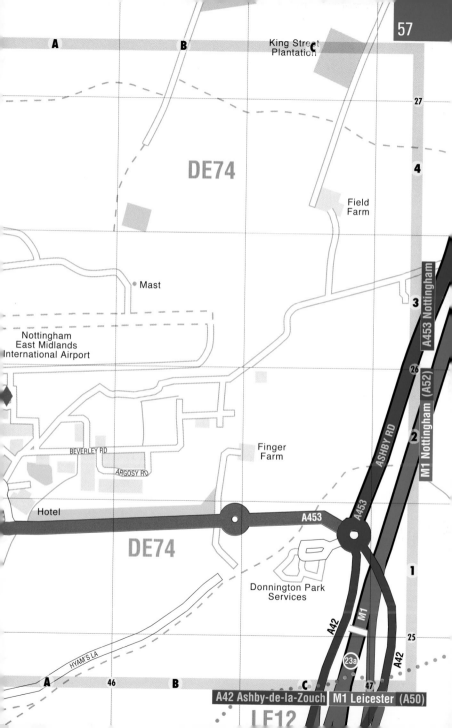

A · B · King Street
Plantation
C

27

DE74

4

Field
Farm

Mast

3

Nottingham
East Midlands
International Airport

A453 Nottingham

26

M1 Nottingham (A52)

2

Finger
Farm

ASHBY RD

BEVERLEY RD

ARGOSY RD

A453

Hotel

A453

DE74

1

Donnington Park
Services

25

HYAM'S LA

A42

M1

A42

23a

A · 46 · B · C · 47

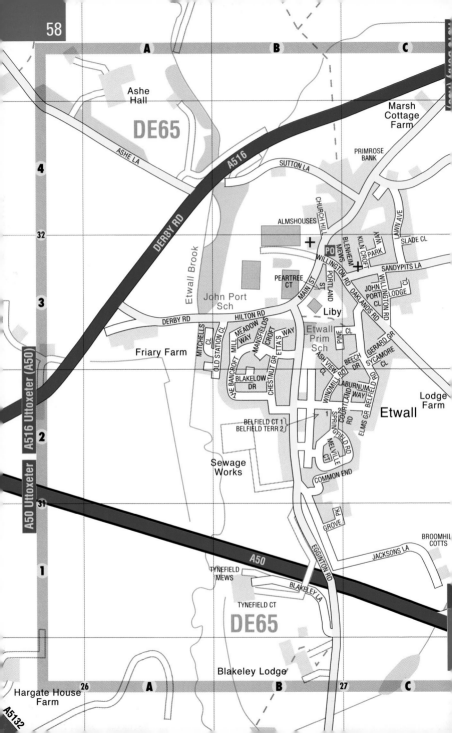

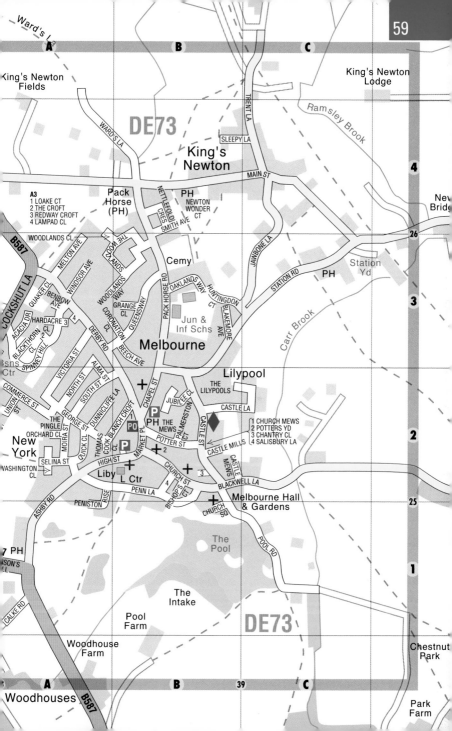

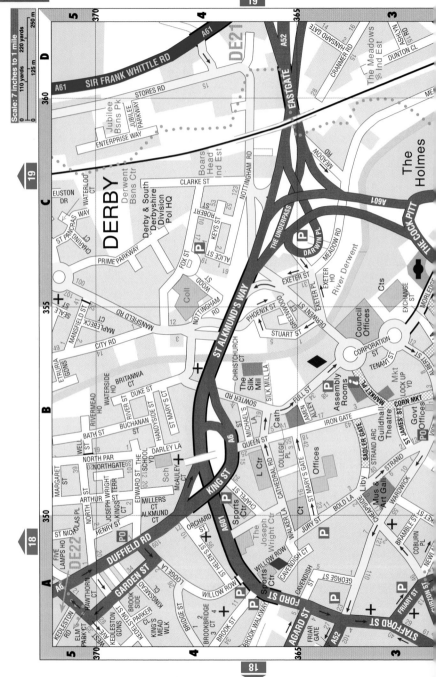

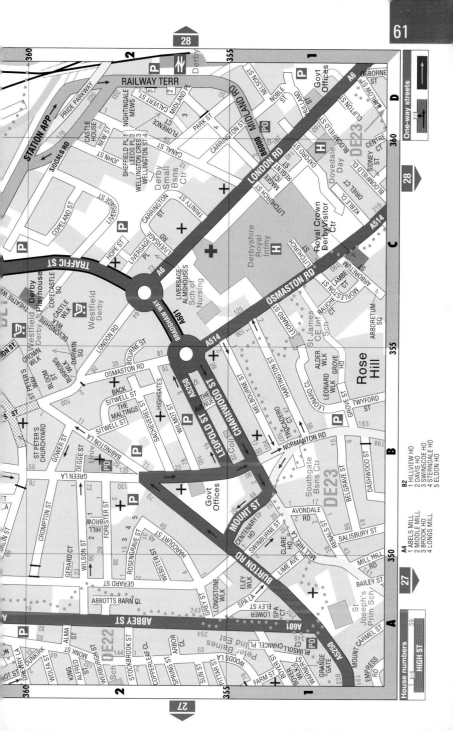

Index

Street names are listed alphabetically and show the locality, the Postcode district, the page number and a reference to
the square in which the name falls on the map page

Maxwell St 5 Paisley PA3..............36 A3

Place name May be abbreviated on the map	**Location number** Present when a number indicates the place's position in a crowded area of mapping	**Locality, town or village** Shown when more than one place has the same name	**Postcode district** District for the indexed place	**Page and grid square** Page number and grid reference for the standard mapping

Towns and villages are listed in CAPITAL LETTERS
Public and commercial buildings are highlighted in magenta. **Places of interest** are highlighted in blue with a star*

Abbreviations used in the index

Acad	**Academy**	Ct	**Court**	Hts	**Heights**	Pl	**Place**
App	**Approach**	Ctr	**Centre**	Ind	**Industrial**	Prec	**Precinct**
Arc	**Arcade**	Ctry	**Country**	Inst	**Institute**	Prom	**Promenade**
Ave	**Avenue**	Cty	**County**	Int	**International**	Rd	**Road**
Bglw	**Bungalow**	Dr	**Drive**	Intc	**Interchange**	Recn	**Recreation**
Bldg	**Building**	Dro	**Drove**	Junc	**Junction**	Ret	**Retail**
Bsns, Bus	**Business**	Ed	**Education**	L	**Leisure**	Sh	**Shopping**
Bvd	**Boulevard**	Emb	**Embankment**	La	**Lane**	Sq	**Square**
Cath	**Cathedral**	Est	**Estate**	Liby	**Library**	St	**Street**
Cir	**Circus**	Ex	**Exhibition**	Mdw	**Meadow**	Sta	**Station**
Cl	**Close**	Gd	**Ground**	Meml	**Memorial**	Terr	**Terrace**
Cnr	**Corner**	Gdn	**Garden**	Mkt	**Market**	TH	**Town Hall**
Coll	**College**	Gn	**Green**	Mus	**Museum**	Univ	**University**
Com	**Community**	Gr	**Grove**	Orch	**Orchard**	Wk, Wlk	**Walk**
Comm	**Common**	H	**Hall**	Pal	**Palace**	Wr	**Water**
Cott	**Cottage**	Ho	**House**	Par	**Parade**	Yd	**Yard**
Cres	**Crescent**	Hospl	**Hospital**	Pas	**Passage**		
Cswy	**Causeway**	HQ	**Headquarters**	Pk	**Park**		

Index of towns, villages, streets, hospitals, industrial estates, railway stations, schools, shopping centres, universities and places of interest

Abb–Alv

A

Abbeydale Cl DE56... **6** C1
Abbeyfields Cl
DE22..............**12** C2
Abbey Hill DE21,
DE22..............**13** A4
Abbey Hill Rd DE22 .**11** C2
Abbey La DE21......**12** C1
Abbey St DE1, DE22..**61** A2
Abbey Yd DE22 ....**12** C1
Abbot Cl DE21 .....**14** A2
Abbot Mews DE22 ..**12** C1
Abbots Gr DE56......**2** C3
Abbotts Barn Cl
DE22..............**61** A2
Abels Mill **1** DE1...**60** A4
Aberdare Cl DE21...**15** A2
Abingdon Bsns Ctr The
DE24..............**28** B1

Abingdon St DE24 .. **37** B4
Abney Cl DE3.......**25** B2
Acacia Ave DE3....**25** A1
Acacia Dr DE73.....**59** A3
Acer Croft DE21 ....**14** A3
Acorn Cl DE24......**47** B3
Acorn Dr DE56......**2** C3
Acorn Way
Belper DE56 ....**2** C3
Derby DE21.........**21** B2
Acrefield Way DE73.. **48** B2
Acresview Cl DE22...**11** C4
Acton Rd DE22 .....**16** B2
Addison Rd DE24 ... **37** B3
Adelaide Cl DE3 ...**25** A4
Adelphi Cl DE23 ...**34** C2
Adler Ct DE1 ......**19** A3
Adrian St DE24 ....**37** C2
Adwick Cl DE3......**24** B2
Agard St DE1......**60** A4
Aimploy Ct DE23....**27** C1
Ainley Cl DE24......**38** B3
Ainsworth Dr DE23 .**36** A3

Airedale Wlk **3**
DE24..............**39** B2
Albany Rd DE22..... **26** B4
Albemarle Rd DE21 .**21** A3
Albert Cres DE21 ...**30** A4
Albert Rd
Breaston DE72......**41** A1
Derby DE21.........**29** C4
Albert St
Belper DE56 ....**2** B2
Derby DE1..........**60** B3
Albion St DE1 .....**61** B3
Albrighton Ave
DE24..............**45** A2
Alder Cl DE21......**14** A3
Alderfen Cl DE24 ...**47** A3
Alderley Ct DE21....**14** C2
Alder Rd DE56.......**2** C1
Aldersgate DE21 ....**16** B3
Alderslade Cl DE72 .**51** B4
Aldersley Cl DE65...**42** C1
Alder Wlk DE23.....**61** B1
Aldwych DE22......**16** C2

Alexandra Gdns **3**
DE23..............**28** A2
Alexandra Mills **2**
DE1..............**18** A1
Alexandre Cl DE23 ..**35** C2
Alfred Rd DE56 .....**6** B2
Alfreton Rd
Breadsall DE21......**13** A2
Little Eaton DE21 ...**10** A2
Alice St DE1.......**60** C4
Alison Cl DE21......**20** B3
Alkmund Ct DE1....**60** B4
Allan Ave DE23 ....**34** A4
Allen St DE24......**38** A1
ALLENTON **37** C1
Allenton Com Prim
Sch DE24...........**37** C1
ALLESTREE.........**12** B3
Allestree Cl DE24 ...**38** A4
Allestree La DE22...**11** C3
Allestree Park*
DE22...............**9** A1
Allestree St DE24 ...**38** B4

All Saints Ct **6**
DE3..............**24** C1
Allstone Lee DE56 ... **2** B3
Alma Hts DE3.......**25** A1
Alma St
Derby DE22.........**61** A2
Melbourne DE73.....**59** A2
Almond St DE23 ...**27** B1
Almshouses DE65...**58** B4
Alonso Cl DE73 ....**47** B2
Alport Cl DE56 ......**3** A3
Alsager Cl DE21 ...**14** C1
Alstonfield Dr DE22 .**11** C3
Alton Cl DE22......**11** C3
Alton Rd DE56 ......**3** B2
Alum Cl DE24......**39** B3
ALVASTON.........**39** A4
Alvaston Inf Sch
DE24..............**39** B3
Alvaston Jun Sch
DE24..............**39** B3
Alvaston Park Homes
DE24..............**29** C1
Alvaston Pk* DE24 **29** B2

Alvaston St DE24 . . . **39** A4
Alverton Cl DE3. . . . **24** B1
Alveston Pk Homes
DE24 . . . . **38** C4
Alward's Cl DE24 . . **38** C2
Ambassador Rd
DE74 . . . . **56** B1
Amber Ct DE56 . . . . . . **2** C4
Amberley Dr DE24 . . **36** B1
Amber Rd DE22 . . . . **11** C1
Amber St DE24 . . . . . **37** B3
Ambervale Cl DE23 . **34** C2
Ambrose Terr DE1 . . **18** A1
Amen Alley DE1 . . . **60** B3
Amesbury La DE21. . **14** A2
Amy St DE22. . . . . . . **27** A4
Anderson St DE14 . . . **38** B2
Andrew Cl DE23 . . . . **34** A4
Anglers' La DE21 . . **31** A3
Anglesey St DE21. . . **19** C4
Anne Potter Cl
DE72 . . . . **23** C1
Anson Rd DE14 . . . . **56** B2
Anstey Ct DE21 . . . . **14** C1
Anthony Cres DE14 . **38** B2
Anthony Dr DE24 . . . **38** B2
Apiary Gate DE74 . . . **53** B1
Appian Cl DE72 . . . . **32** B1
Appian Way DE24. . . **39** C1
Applecross Ct DE24 . **45** B3
Appledore Dr DE21 . **15** A1
Appledown Way
DE23 . . . . **34** C2
Applegate Cl DE21. . **15** A3
Applemead Cl DE21 . **14** A2
Appleton Cl DE21 . . **20** C3
Appleton Dr DE56. . . **3** A4
Appletree Cl DE72 . . **32** B2
Appletree Wlk DE3 . **24** C2
Applewood Cl DE56 . . . **3** A3
Arbor Cl DE22 . . . . . **61** A2
Arboretum Pk*
DE23 . . . . **28** A3
Arboretum Prim Sch
DE23 . . . . **27** C2
Arboretum Sq
DE23 . . . . **61** C1
Arboretum St DE23 . **61** C1
Archer St DE24 . . . . . **29** A2
Arden Cl DE23 . . . . . **27** A2
Ardleigh Cl DE3 . . . **33** C4
Argosy Rd DE74. . . . **57** B2
Argyle St DE22. . . . . **27** B3
Argyll Cl DE21 . . . . . **22** B1
Arkendale Wlk 4
DE24 . . . . **39** B2
Arkle Gn DE24 . . . . **45** B4
Arkwright Ave DE56. . **3** B4
Arkwright St DE24 . . **37** B3
Arleston La DE24 . . **45** A2
Arleston St DE23. . . **36** B3
Arlington Dr DE24 . . **38** B2
Arlington Rd DE23 . **26** C2
Armscote Cl DE3 . . **15** A2
Arnhem Terr DE1 . . **31** B3
Arnold St DE22 . . . . **17** C1
Arran Cl DE24 . . . . **45** B3
Arreton Cl DE24 . . . **39** B1
Arridge Rd DE21 . . **20** B2
Arthur Cl 1 DE23. . **28** A2
Arthur Hind Cl
DE22 . . . . **18** B3
Arthur St
Derby DE1. . . . . **60** B5
Draycott DE72 . . . . . **40** B2
Arundel Ave DE24 . . **25** B2
Arundel Dr DE21. . . **22** B1
Arundel St DE22 . . **26** C4

Ascot Dr DE24 . . . . . **37** C4
Ash Acre DE56. . . . . . **3** C2
Ashberry Ct DE22 . . **12** C4
Ashbourne Ct DE22 . **18** A2
Ashbourne Rd
Derby DE22. . . . . **17** B3
Mackworth DE22 . . . . **16** A4
Ashbrook Ave DE72 . **32** B2
Ashbrook Cl DE22. . **11** B3
Ashbrook Inf Sch
DE72 . . . . **32** A2
Ashbrook Jun Sch
DE72 . . . . **32** A2
Ashby Rd
Diseworth DE74 . . . . **56** C1
Melbourne DE73 . . . . **59** A1
Ashby St DE14 . . . . **38** A2
Ash Cl
Aston-on-T DE72. . . . **51** B2
Derby DE22. . . . . **11** C4
Ashcombe Gdns
DE21 . . . . **15** A1
Ashcroft Cl DE24 . . **38** C3
Ash Croft Prim Sch
DE24 . . . . **45** B2
Ashdene Gdns DE56 . **3** B3
Ashe La DE65. . . . . . **58** A4
Ashe Pl DE23 . . . . . **27** B1
Ashfield Ave DE21 . . **20** A4
Ashford Rise DE56 . . **3** B4
Ashgate Prim Sch
DE22 . . . . **17** C2
Ashgrove Ct DE21 . . **15** A1
Ashleigh Dr DE73 . . **47** C2
Ashley St DE22 . . . . **17** B1
Ashlyn Rd DE21. . . . **19** B1
Ashmeadow DE72 . . **32** A1
Ashop Rd DE56 . . . . . **3** C3
Ashopton Ave DE23 . **36** B4
Ashover Cl DE21 . . . **20** B4
Ashover Rd
1 Derby, Chaddesden
DE21 . . . . **20** A4
Derby DE22. . . . . **11** C2
Ashton Cl DE3 . . . . **24** B3
Ashton Way DE56. . . . **3** C2
Ashtree Ave DE24 . . **37** A2
Ash Tree Cl
Breadsall DE21. . . . . **14** A4
Duffield DE56 . . . . **7** B4
Ash View Cl DE65 . . **58** B2
Ashworth Ave DE21. **20** B1
Ashworth Wlk DE21. **20** B1
Askerfield Ave
DE22 . . . . **11** B4
Aspen Bsns Ctr
DE21 . . . . **30** A4
Aspen Dr DE21 . . . . **30** B4
Asterdale Prim Sch
DE21 . . . . **31** B3
Asterdale View
DE21 . . . . **31** B4
Aster Gdns DE23. . . **35** A3
Astlow Dr DE56 . . . . . **3** A4
Aston Cl DE3 . . . . . **50** C4
Aston Hall Dr DE72 . **51** A2
Aston Hall Hospl
DE72 . . . . **51** A1
Aston La DE73 . . . . **48** B1
ASTON-ON-
TRENT **51** B3
Aston-on-Trent Prim
Sch DE72 . . . . **51** A3
Aston Rd DE23. . . . . **35** B1
Astorville Park Rd
DE73 . . . . **47** C2

Atchison Gdns
DE21 . . . . **21** A3
Atherfield Wlk
DE24 . . . . **39** B1
Athlone Cl DE21 . . . **19** C4
Athol Cl DE24. . . . . . **45** B4
Atlow Rd DE21. . . . . **20** A3
Attewell Cl DE72. . . **41** A1
Attlebridge Cl DE21 **19** C4
Atwall Ct DE21. . . . . **27** C1
Atworth Gr DE23. . . **34** B3
Auckland Cl DE3 . . **25** B3
Audley Ctr DE1 . . . **60** B3
Audrey Dr DE21. . . . **20** C4
Augusta St DE23 . . **28** A2
Aults Cl DE65 . . . . . **42** C1
Austen Ave DE23. . . **35** A4
Austin Sq DE23 . . . **36** B3
Autumn Gr DE21. . . **20** B1
Avalon Dr DE73 . . . **50** B4
Avenue Rd DE56 . . . . **7** B4
Avenue The
Belper DE56 . . . . **4** A4
Derby, Chaddesden
DE21 . . . . **20** B1
Derby DE1. . . . . **61** B2
Averham Cl DE21 . . **15** A1
Aviemore Way
DE24. . . . . **45** B4
Avocet Ct DE24 . . . . **45** A4
Avon Cl DE24 . . . . . **45** A2
Avondale Rd
Derby DE23. . . . . **61** B1
Derby, Spondon
DE21 . . . . **21** C2
Avonmouth Dr
DE24. . . . . **38** A4
Avon St DE24 . . . . . **38** A4
Aycliffe Gdns DE24 . **47** C4
Aylesbury Ave DE21 . **20** B3
Ayr Cl DE21. . . . . . . **30** C4

Column B

B

Babbacombe Cl
DE24 . . . . **39** B3
Babington Bsns Coll
DE1 . . . . **61** B1
Babington Hospl
DE56 . . . . **4** A4
Babington La DE1 . . **61** B2
Back La
Castle Donington
DE74 . . . . **53** A3
Chellaston DE73. . . . **48** A2
Back Sitwell St DE1. **61** B2
Back Wyver La DE56 . **2** B3
Badger Cl DE21. . . . **22** B2
Badgerdale DE23 . . **34** C3
Bagshaw St DE24 . . **38** A4
Bailey St DE23 . . . . **61** A1
Bainbridge St DE23 **27** C3
Bains Dr DE72 . . . . . **32** C1
Bakeacre La DE65 . . **43** B3
Bakehouse La DE72 . **23** B1
Baker St DE24 . . . . . **38** B4
Bakewell Cl DE3 . . **25** A3
Bakewell Dr DE74. . **56** A4
Bakewell St DE22 . . **27** B4
Balaclava Rd DE23 . **36** A4
Balfour Rd DE23 . . **36** C4
Balgonie Ct DE73 . . **47** B2
Balham Wlk DE22 . . **16** C2
Ballards Way DE72. . **32** C1
Ballater Cl DE24 . . **45** B4
Balleny Cl DE21. . . . **14** B2
Balmoral Cl DE23 . **26** A2
Balmoral Rd DE72 . **32** B1

Bamburgh Cl DE21. **30** C4
Bamford Ave DE23 . **36** B4
Bancroft Dr DE22 . . **11** B4
Bancroft The DE65. . **58** B2
Bangor St DE21. . . . **20** A4
Bank Bldgs DE56 . . . **4** A1
Bank Ct DE22. . . . . . **18** A4
Bankfield Dr DE21 . **31** B4
Bankholmes Cl
DE24. . . . . **45** B2
Bank Side DE22. . . . **12** A2
Bank View Rd DE22 . **18** B4
Bannels Ave DE23 . **35** A3
Banwell Cl DE3 . . . **24** B3
Barcheston Cl
DE21 . . . . **15** A2
Barden Dr DE22 . . . **12** B3
Bardsey Ct DE21 . . **15** A3
Bare La DE72 . . . . . . **23** B1
Barf Cl DE3. . . . . **25** A1
BARGATE **5** A3
Bargate Cl DE56 . . . . **5** A3
Bargate Rd DE56 . . . . **4** C3
Barley Cft DE73. . . . **47** C1
Barley Cl DE21. . . . . **10** A4
Barley Corn Cl
DE21 . . . . **15** B2
Barley Croft DE56. . . **4** C4
Barlow St DE1,
DE23 . . . . **61** D1
Barnard Rd DE21 . . **13** C2
Barn Cl
Castle Donington
DE74 . . . . **53** B1
Findern DE65 . . . . . . **43** A2
Quarndon DE22 . . . . . **8** A2
Barn Croft DE23 . . . **26** B1
Barnes Gn DE22 . . . **17** A3
Barnhill Gr DE23. . . **34** C3
Barnstaple Cl DE21 . **14** C2
Barnwood Cl DE21. . **24** B2
Baron Cl DE21 . . . . **15** C3
Barrett St DE24 . . . **38** C3
Barrie Dr DE24 . . . . **36** B1
Barron's Way DE72 . **32** B1
Barroon DE74 . . . . . **53** B1
Barton Cl DE21 . . . . **22** B2
Barton Knowle DE56. **3** C2
Basildon Cl DE24 . . **38** B1
Baslow Dr DE22 . . . **12** B3
Bassingham Cl
DE21 . . . . **15** A1
Bass St DE22 . . . . . **17** C2
Bateman St DE23 . . **28** B3
Bath Rd DE3 . . . . . . **25** A2
Bath St DE1 . . . . . . **60** B5
Baverstock Cl DE73 **47** C3
Baxter Sq DE23 . . . **36** B2
Bayleaf Cres DE21 . **15** A3
Bayswater Cl DE22. . **16** B2
Beackden Cl DE56 . . **3** D2
Beaconfields Ho
DE21 . . . . **30** A4
Beamwood Cl 3
DE21 . . . . **14** B1
Beardmore Cl DE21 . **14** B2
Beatty St DE24. . . . . **38** B4
Beaufort Com Prim
Sch DE21 . . . . **19** B4
Beaufort Court Ind Est
DE21 . . . . **19** B4
Beaufort Rd DE24. . **45** A2
Beaufort St DE21 . . **19** C3
Beaumaris Ct DE21 . **22** B1
Beaumont Cl DE56 . . **3** C2
Beaumont Wlk
DE23 . . . . **36** A2

Beaurepaire Cres
DE56. . . . . **3** A3
Beaureper Ave
DE22 . . . . **12** A3
Becher St DE23 . . . **27** C1
Beckenham Way
DE22 . . . . **17** A2
Becket Prim Sch
DE22 . . . . **27** B4
Becket St DE1 . . . . **60** A3
Becket Well La DE1 . **61** B3
Beckitt Cl DE24 . . . **38** C4
Becksitch La DE56 . . **4** A4
Beckstich Ct DE56 . . **4** A3
Bedford Cl DE22 . . **26** C3
Bedford St DE22 . . **26** C3
Beech Ave
Borrowash DE72. . . . **32** B3
Derby DE24. . . . . **39** A3
Melbourne DE73 . . . **59** B3
Beech Cl
Belper DE56 . . . . **2** C1
Kilburn DE56. . . . . **6** C2
Beechcroft DE21. . . **13** C4
Beech Ct DE21 . . . . **21** C1
Beech Dr
Derby DE22. . . . . **18** B4
Etwall DE65 . . . . **58** C3
Findern DE65 . . . . . . **43** B1
Beeches Ave DE21 . **21** C1
Beech Gdns DE24 . . **39** A3
Beechley Dr DE21. . **15** A1
Beech Wlk DE23 . . **26** C1
Beechwood Cl DE56 . **2** A3
Beechwood Cres
DE23 . . . . **35** B4
Beechwood Ct
DE23 . . . . **28** A3
Beechwood Park Dr
DE22 . . . . **12** B1
Beeley Cl
Belper DE56 . . . . **3** B4
Derby DE22. . . . . **11** C2
Derby, Oakwood
DE21 . . . . **14** B2
Belfast Wlk DE21 . . **29** C4
Belfield Ct DE65 . . **58** B2
Belfield Rd DE65. . . **58** C2
Belfield Terr DE65. . **58** B2
Belfry Cl DE3 . . . . . **25** B1
Belgrave Cl DE56 . . . **3** B3
Belgrave St DE23 . . **61** B1
Bell Ave DE72. . . . . . **51** B2
Belle Acre Cl 3
DE56 . . . . **2** B1
Bellingham Ct
DE22 . . . . **11** B2
Belmont Dr DE72 . . **32** A1
Belpar Ho DE21. . . . **31** A3
BELPER **3** A1
Belper La DE56 . . . . . **2** A4
Belper Rd
3 Derby DE22. . . . . **18** B3
Holbrook DE56. . . . . . **5** A2
Kilburn DE56. . . . . **5** C4
Belper Sch DE56 . . . **3** C2
Belper Sta DE56 . . . . **2** B2
Belsize Ct DE22 . . . **16** B2
Belvedere Cl DE3 . . **24** C3
Belvoir Cl DE21 . . . **41** C1
Belvoir St DE23 . . . **27** B1
Bembridge Dr DE24. **39** B1
Bemrose Com Sch
DE22 . . . . **26** C4

Bemrose Mews DE22 26 B4
Bemrose Rd DE24 38 A3
Benbow Ave DE73 59 A3
Bendall Gn DE23 35 B1
Benmore Ct DE21 15 A3
Bennett St DE24 37 C1
Bensley Cl DE73 48 A1
Benson St DE24 38 B3
Bentley Rd DE74 52 C2
Bentley St DE24 38 A2
Beresford Dr DE21 31 A4
Berkeley Cl DE23 35 C3
Berkshire St DE21 19 C4
Bermuda Ave DE21 10 A2
Berry Park Cl DE22 12 A1
Berwick Ave DE21 19 B3
Berwick Cl DE24 39 A1
Berwick Dr DE24 45 A3
Bessalone Dr DE56 2 C4
Besthorpe Cl DE21 15 A1
Bethulie Rd DE23 36 C4
Betjeman Sq DE24 36 C1
Beverley Rd DE74 57 A2
Beverley St DE24 28 C2
Bewdley Cl DE73 48 A3
Bexhill Wlk DE21 14 A1
Bicester Ave DE24 44 C2
Bickley Moss DE21 15 A1
Bideford Dr DE23 35 C2
Biggin The DE74 53 B1
Bilberry Cl DE21 14 B1
Bingham St DE24 38 A2
Binscombe La DE21 14 B3
Birch Cl DE21 22 C2
Birches Rd DE22 11 C4
Birchfield Cl DE73 47 C2
Birchover Ho
1 Derby, Allestree DE22 12 B3
Derby, Markeaton DE22 17 C4
Birchover Rise DE21 14 B1
Birchover Way DE22 12 A2
Birch Vale DE56 2 B3
Birchview Cl DE56 4 C4
Birch View Ct DE1 18 B3
Birchway Gr DE23 34 C2
Birchwood Ave DE23 35 C2
Birdcage Wlk DE22 16 B2
Birdwood St DE23 27 B1
Birkdale Cl DE3 25 C2
Biscay Ct DE21 15 B2
Bishop Lonsdale CE Prim Sch DE22 27 A3
Bishops Ct DE73 59 B2
Bishop's Ct DE73 59 A2
Bishop's Dr DE21 14 A2
Bishop's Gn DE22 26 C3
Blaby Cl DE23 36 A2
Blackberry Way DE56 6 A4
Blackbird Row DE56 5 A3
Blackmore St DE23 36 B3
Blackmount Ct 5 DE24 45 A3
Blackthorn Cl
Derby DE21 14 A2
Melbourne DE73 59 A3
Blackthorne Cl DE56 6 A4
Blackwell La DE73 59 A2
Blagreaves Ave DE23 35 B1
Blagreaves La DE23 35 B2
Blair Ho DE23 35 B1
Blakebrook Dr DE73 48 A3
Blakeley La DE65 58 B1
Blakelow Dr DE65 58 B2
Blakemore Ave DE73 59 B3
Blakeney Ct DE21 15 B1
Blanch Croft DE73 59 B2
Blandford Cl DE24 39 C2
Blankney Cl DE24 45 A2
Blencathra Dr DE3 34 A4
Blenheim Ct DE56 3 C3
Blenheim Dr DE22 11 C4
Blenheim Mews DE65 58 C3
Blenheim Par DE22 11 C4
Blind La DE72 41 C2
Blithfield Gdns DE73 48 A2
Bloomfield Cl DE1 61 C1
Bloomfield St DE1 61 D1
Bloom St DE1 61 B2
Bluebell Cl DE24 45 A2
Bluebird Ct DE24 45 A4
Blyth Ct DE74 53 B2
Blyth Pl DE21 13 C1
Boars Head Ind Est DE1 60 C4
Bobbin Way DE56 3 B3
Boden St DE23 28 A2
Bodmin Cl DE24 45 A3
Bold La DE1 60 B3
Bonchurch Cl DE24 39 B1
Bondgate DE74 53 B1
Bonnyrigg Dr DE21 14 C2
Bonsall Ave DE23 35 C4
Bonsall Dr DE3 25 A3
Booth St DE24 38 B3
Border Cres DE24 39 A1
Borough St DE74 53 B1
BORROWASH 32 B2
Borrowash By-pass DE72 32 B3
Borrowash Rd DE21 31 B4
Borrowfield Rd DE21 31 B3
Borrowfields DE72 32 A1
Borrow Wood Inf Sch DE21 22 B1
Borrow Wood Jun Sch DE21 22 B1
Boscastle Rd DE24 39 A2
Bosley Mews DE56 2 B3
Boston Cl DE21 21 B2
Boswell Sq DE23 36 B3
Bosworth Ave DE23 36 A2
Bosworth Rd DE74 52 C1
Bottlebrook Houses DE5 6 C3
BOULTON 39 A2
Boulton Dr DE24 38 C2
Boulton La
Derby, Allenton DE24 38 B1
Derby DE24 38 C2
Boulton Prim Sch DE24 38 C2
Boundary Rd DE22 27 A4
Bourne St DE1 61 B2
Bowbank Cl DE23 34 C2
Bowbridge Ave DE23 35 B1
Bower St DE24 38 B4
Bowland Cl DE3 25 A1
Bowlees Ct DE23 34 A3
Bowler Dr DE56 6 B1
Bowmer Rd DE24 29 A1
Bown Cl DE56 6 B2
Boxmoor Cl DE23 34 B3
Boyd Gr DE73 50 C4
Boyer St DE22 61 A1
Boyer Wlk DE22 61 A1
Boylestone Rd DE23 35 B1
Brackens Ave DE24 38 B1
Brackensdale Ave DE22 17 A1
Brackensdale Inf Sch DE22 17 A2
Brackensdale Jun Sch DE22 17 A2
Bracken's La DE24 38 B2
Brackley DE56 6 A3
Brackley Dr DE21 22 A1
Bracknell Dr DE24 38 B1
Bradbourne Ct DE22 27 A3
Bradbury Cl DE72 32 B1
Bradgate Ct DE23 36 A2
Brading Cl DE24 39 C1
Bradley Dr DE56 3 A2
Bradley St DE22 18 A4
Bradmoor Gr DE73 48 B2
Bradshaw Croft DE56 2 A4
Bradshaw Dr DE56 5 A1
Bradshaw Way DE1 61 C2
Bradwell Cl DE3 25 A1
Bradwell Way DE56 3 A3
Braeburn Ct DE23 27 A2
Braemar Cl 11 DE24 45 A3
Brafield Cl DE56 3 C2
Brailsford Rd DE21 20 B4
Braintree Cl DE21 13 C2
Braithwell Cl DE22 12 B2
Brambleberry Ct DE21 15 A3
Bramble Mews 2 DE3 24 C1
Bramble St DE1 60 A3
Bramble Way DE56 6 A4
Bramblewick Dr DE23 34 C2
Brambling Cres DE3 33 A2
Bramfield Ave DE22 27 A3
Bramfield Ct DE22 27 A4
Bramley Cl DE21 15 B3
Brampton Cl DE3 24 B3
Brampton Ct DE56 3 C2
Brandelhow Ct DE21 15 B3
Branksome Ave DE24 39 B3
Brassington Rd DE21 14 B1
Brayfield Ave DE23 35 C4
Brayfield Rd DE23 35 B4
BREADSALL 14 A4
Breadsall CE Prim Sch DE21 14 A4
BREADSALL HILLTOP 13 C2
Breadsall Hill Top Inf Sch DE21 14 A1
Breadsall Hill Top Jun Sch DE21 14 A1
BREASTON 41 C1
Breaston Ind Est DE72 41 B1
Brecon Cl DE21 22 A2
Breedon Ave DE23 35 C1
Breedon Hill Rd DE23 27 B3
Brendan Gdns DE22 12 A1
Brentford Dr DE22 17 A2
Bretby Sq DE23 35 B1
Bretton Ave DE23 26 B2
Bretton Rd DE56 3 D3
Breydon Cl DE24 47 A4
Brian Clough Way DE21 30 B4
Briar Cl
Borrowash DE72 32 B2
Derby DE21 21 A1
Briar Lea Cl DE24 45 C4
Briarsgate DE22 11 C2
Briarwood Way DE23 35 B2
Brick Row DE22 12 C1
Brick St DE1 18 A2
Brickyard La DE56 6 A4
Bridge Field DE72 41 B1
Bridgefield Ct 11 DE56 2 B2
Bridge Foot DE56 2 B3
Bridge Hill DE56 2 A3
Bridgend Ct DE21 15 B2
Bridgeness Rd DE23 34 B2
Bridgeport Rd DE21 21 B2
Bridge St
Belper DE56 2 B2
Derby DE1 60 A4
Bridge View DE56 4 B1
Bridgwater Cl DE24 39 B3
Bridle Cl DE73 48 A1
Brierfield Way DE3 34 A4
Brigden Ave DE24 38 A3
Brighstone Cl DE24 39 B1
Brighton Rd DE24 38 B4
Bright St DE22 17 C1
Brigmor Wlk DE22 17 B1
Brindle Way DE23 34 C1
Brindley Wlk DE24 45 B2
Brisbane Rd DE3 25 B3
Briset Cl DE24 45 B2
Bristol Dr DE3 25 A2
Britannia Ct DE1 60 B4
Broad Bank DE22 18 A4
Broadfields Cl DE22 18 B4
Broad La DE72 49 C4
Broadleaf Cl DE21 14 A2
Broad Rushes DE74 53 B4
Broadstone Cl DE21 14 C1
Broadway
Derby DE22 18 A4
Duffield DE56 7 B1
Broadway Park Cl DE22 18 A4
Brockley DE21 22 A1
Brodie Cl DE73 47 B2
Bromley St DE22 18 A3
Brompton Rd DE22 16 B2
Bromyard Dr DE73 48 A3
Bronte Pl DE23 35 A4
Brookbridge Ct DE1 60 A4
Brook Cl
5 Belper DE56 2 B1
Findern DE65 43 A1
Quarndon DE22 11 B4
Brook Ct DE72 49 C4
Brookdale Dr DE23 34 C1
Brookfield Ave
Derby, Chaddesden DE21 21 A4
Derby, Littleover DE23 35 C2
Brookfield Prim Sch DE3 33 C4
Brookfields DE56 5 C1
Brookfields Dr DE21 13 C4
Brook Ho 3 DE1 60 A4
Brookhouse St DE24 37 C1
Brooklands Dr DE23 35 B4
Brook Rd
Borrowash DE72 32 A1
Elvaston DE72 49 C4
Brooks Hollow DE21 10 A3
Brookside DE1 60 A4
Brook Side DE56 2 B1
Brookside Cl DE1 18 A3
Brookside Rd DE21 14 A4
Brook St DE1 60 A4
Brookvale Ave DE5 6 B4
Brookvale Rd DE5 6 B4
Brookvale Rise DE5 6 B4
Brook Walkway DE1 60 A4
Broom Cl
Belper DE56 2 A4
Chellaston DE73 47 C2
Derby, Sinfin DE73 45 B2
Duffield DE56 7 A2
Broomhill Cl DE3 24 C3
Broomhill Cotts DE65 58 C1
Brough St DE22 17 C1
Broughton Ave DE23 26 C1
Browning Cir DE23 36 B3
Browning St DE23 36 B3
Brown's La DE56 5 B1
Brunel Parkway DE24 28 C3
Brunswick St DE23 36 B4
Brunswood Cl DE21 22 A1
Brunton Cl DE3 24 B1
Bryony Cl DE21 14 C1
Buchanan St DE1 60 B4
Buchan St DE24 37 C3
Buckingham Ave DE21 19 C4
Buckland Cl DE1 18 A2
Buckminster Cl DE21 14 B2
Buller St DE23 27 A2
Bullpit La DE56 9 B4
Bullsmoor DE56 3 B2
Bunting Cl DE3 25 C3
Burbage Cl DE56 3 C3
Burbage Pl DE24 38 B3
Burdock Cl DE21 14 A2
Burghley Cl DE73 47 C2
Burghley Way DE23 34 A2
Burleigh Dr DE22 18 B4
Burley Dr DE22 8 C3
Burley Hill DE22 9 B3
Burley La DE22 8 C3
Burlington Cl DE72 41 C2
Burlington Rd DE22 16 B2
Burlington Way DE3 24 C1
Burnaby St DE24 38 B4
Burnage Ct DE22 27 B4

Burnham Dr DE3 ... 24 B2
Burns Cl DE3 ..... 35 A4
Burnside Cl DE24 ... 45 A3
Burnside Ct DE24 ... 38 C4
Burnside Dr DE21... 31 B4
Burnside St DE24 ... 38 C4
Burrowfield Mews
  DE21 .... 31 B2
Burrows Wlk DE1... 61 B2
Burton Rd
  Derby DE23........ 26 B1
  Findern DE65 .... 43 A4
Bute Wlk DE21...... 19 B3
Buttermere Dr
  DE22 .... 12 A3
Butterwick Cl DE23. 36 A1
Buttonoak Dr DE73. 48 A3
Butts The DE3...... 2 C1
Buxton Dr DE3..... 25 A3
Buxton Rd DE21 .... 20 B4
Byfield Cl DE21 .... 15 A2
Byng Ave DE23 ..... 36 B3
Byron St DE23 ..... 27 B2
Bywell La DE56..... 6 A3

C

Cabot Cl DE56 ...... 3 D3
Cadgwith Dr DE22 .. 12 A3
Cadwell Cl DE24 ... 39 C2
Caerhays Ct DE24... 45 A3
Caernarvon Cl
  DE21 .... 22 B1
Caesar St DE1 ..... 19 A3
Cairngorm Dr DE23 45 A3
Cairns Cl DE3 ..... 25 A3
Calder Cl DE22 .... 12 A3
Caldermill Dr DE21 .14 C2
CALIFORNIA 26 C3
California Gdns
  DE22 .... 26 B4
Calke Rd DE73..... 59 A1
Callow Hill Way
  DE23 .... 34 C3
Calver Cl
  Belper DE56 ...... 3 A4
  Derby DE21....... 14 A3
Calverton Cl DE24 . 47 B3
Calvert St DE1 ..... 61 D2
Calvin Cl DE24..... 38 C1
Camberwell Ave
  DE22 .... 16 C2
Camborne Cl DE21..14 A2
Cambridge St
  Derby, Rose Hill
  DE23 ....28 A2
  Derby, Spondon
  DE21 ....31 A3
Camden St DE22... 26 C4
Camellia Cl DE3 ... 24 C3
Cameron Rd DE23 .. 36 B4
Campbell St
  Belper DE56 ...... 2 B1
  Derby DE24........ 37 C3
Campion Hill DE74.. 53 A2
Campion St DE22 ... 17 C1
Campsie Ct 8
  DE24 .... 45 A3
Camp St DE1 ..... 19 A3
Camp Wood Close
  DE21 .... 10 A3
Canada St DE56 .... 4 B4
Canalgate Pk DE1 . 31 B3
Canal St DE1 ..... 61 C2
Canberra Cl DE3... 25 A2
Canon's Wlk DE21 . 12 B2
Canterbury Cl DE56.. 7 B2
Canterbury St DE21 20 A4

Cantley Cl DE24..... 47 A3
Cardales Cl DE65 ... 43 A2
Cardean Cl DE1..... 19 A3
Cardigan St DE21 ... 19 C3
Cardinal Cl 1 DE1 14 B2
Cardrona Cl DE21...14 B2
Carisbrooke Gdns
  DE23 .... 35 B2
Carlisle Ave DE23... 35 A4
Carlton Ave DE24 ... 47 B4
Carlton Dr DE24 .... 47 B3
Carlton Gdns DE24.. 47 B4
Carlton Rd DE23.... 27 A2
Carlton Walk DE24.. 29 C1
Carlton Wlk DE24... 38 C4
Carlyle Inf Sch
  DE23 .... 35 A4
Carlyle St DE24 .... 36 B1
Carnaby Cl DE22....16 C1
Carnegie St DE23 ... 36 C4
Carnforth Cl DE3 ... 25 A1
Carnival Way DE74.. 53 B2
Carnoustie Cl DE3 .. 25 B2
Carol Cres DE21 .... 20 B1
Caroline Cl DE24.... 39 C3
Carradale Gr DE73.. 47 B1
Carrington Ct Ind Est
  DE1 .... 18 A1
Carrington St DE1 .. 61 C2
Carron Cl DE24 .... 45 B4
Carrs Cl DE74....... 53 A1
Carsington Cres
  DE22 .... 11 C1
Carsington Ho 1
  DE22 .... 11 C2
Carsington Mews
  DE22 .... 12 A1
Carson Rd DE21 .... 21 A2
Carter St DE24...... 37 C2
Cascade Gr DE23 ... 34 C3
Casson Ave DE24 ... 38 C2
Castings Rd DE24 ... 37 A4
Castle Cl DE72...... 32 C2
Castlecraig Ct DE24. 45 B2
Castle Croft DE1.... 39 C1
CASTLE
  DONINGTON 53 C1
Castle Donington Com
  Coll DE74..........53 B1
Castle Hill
  Castle Donington
  DE74 ....53 B2
  Duffield DE56 .... 7 B3
  Findern DE65 .... 43 A1
Castle Ho DE1 ...... 61 D2
Castle La DE73 ..... 59 A2
Castleland Way
  DE73 .... 47 B2
Castle Mews DE73.. 59 B2
Castle Mills DE73 ... 59 B2
Castle Orch DE56 ... 7 B3
Castleshaw Dr
  DE23 .... 34 A3
Castle St DE73...... 59 B2
Castleton Ave DE23. 36 B4
Castle View DE1..... 61 C2
Castle Wlk DE1 ..... 61 C2
Cathedral Rd DE1... 60 B4
Cathedral View
  DE22 .... 26 C2
Catherine McAuley Ho
  DE22 .... 12 A1
Catherine St DE23 .. 28 A2
Cath of All Saints,
  Derby ★ DE1....... 60 B4
Catterick Dr DE3 ... 24 B1
Causeway DE22.....12 A2
Cavan Dr DE21......30 A3

Cavendish Ave
  DE22 .... 12 B3
Cavendish Cl
  Castle Donington
  DE74 ....56 A4
  Duffield DE56 .... 7 A1
Cavendish Close Inf
  Sch DE21..........20 C4
Cavendish Close Jun
  Sch DE21..........21 A4
Cavendish Ct DE1... 60 A4
Cavendish St DE1... 60 A3
Cavendish Way
  DE3 .... 25 A2
Caversfield Cl DE23 34 C4
Caxton Ct DE23 ..... 36 A2
Caxton St
  Derby DE23........ 36 B2
  Derby, Normanton
  DE23 ....36 A3
Cecil St DE22 ...... 17 C2
Cedar Cl DE56 ...... 7 A1
Cedar Croft
  Aston-on-T DE72...51 A2
  Kilburn DE56........ 6 C1
Cedar Dr DE72...... 32 B4
Cedar Gr DE56...... 7 A1
Cedar Rd DE74 ..... 56 B4
Cedar St DE22 ..... 18 A4
Cedarwood Ct
  DE21 .... 14 C2
Celandine Cl DE21...14 C2
Celanese Rd DE21.. 30 B3
Cemetery Hill DE21. 20 A2
Cemetery Rd DE56... 2 C3
Centenary Ho DE1 .. 61 B1
Central Ave DE72 ... 32 A1
Centre Ct DE1 ..... 61 C1
Centro Pl DE24 ..... 28 C3
Centurion Way Bsns
  Pk DE21...........19 A4
CHADDESDEN ... 20 A3
Chaddesden La
  DE21 .... 20 B2
Chaddesden Lane End
  DE21 .... 20 B2
Chaddesden Park Inf
  Sch DE21..........21 A2
Chaddesden Park Jun
  Sch DE21..........21 A2
Chaddesden Park Rd
  DE21 .... 20 B3
Chadfield Rd DE56... 7 B4
Chadwick Ave
  DE24 .... 38 A1
Chaffinch Cl DE21 .. 22 B2
Chain La DE3 ...... 25 C2
Chalfont Sq DE21... 15 A2
Chalkley Cl DE24... 38 B3
Challis Ave DE21... 14 C2
Chambers St DE24.. 29 B1
Champion Hill DE56. 7 B3
Chancel Pl DE22.... 61 A1
Chancery La DE22 .. 16 C2
Chandlers Ford
  DE21 .... 14 B2
Chandos Pole St
  DE22 .... 17 C2
Chandres Ct DE22 .. 12 A4
Chantry Cl
  Derby DE3......... 24 B1
  Melbourne DE73...59 A2
Chapel La
  Chellaston DE73....48 A1
  Derby, Chaddesden
  DE21 ....20 C3
  Derby, Spondon
  DE21 .... 22 A1

Chapel Row DE72...32 A2
Chapel Side DE21... 22 A1
Chapel St
  Belper DE56 .... 2 B1
  Derby DE1......... 60 B4
  Derby, Spondon
  DE21 .... 22 A1
  Duffield DE56 .... 7 C2
  Holbrook DE56 ...... 5 A1
  Kilburn DE56........ 6 B2
  Melbourne DE73...59 B2
Chapman Ave DE24 39 A2
Chapter Cl DE21 ... 13 C2
Charing Ct DE1 .... 60 C5
Charingworth Rd
  DE21 .... 15 A2
Chariot Cl DE24.... 39 C1
Charlbury Ct DE23 . 34 C4
Charles Ave DE21 .. 21 C2
Charles Rd DE24 ... 29 C1
Charleston Rd
  DE21 .... 21 B2
Charlestown Dr
  DE22 .... 11 C4
Charlotte St DE23... 27 C2
Charnwood Ave
  Belper DE56 .... 2 C2
  Borrowash DE72...32 B2
  Castle Donington
  DE74 ....53 C1
  Derby DE23........ 35 C1
Charnwood St DE1.. 61 B2
Charterhouse Cl
  DE21 .... 14 B3
Charterstone La
  DE22 .... 12 A4
Chartwell Dr DE21 .. 19 B1
Chase Cl DE73...... 48 B2
Chase The
  Derby DE24........ 45 C4
  Kilburn DE56........ 6 C2
Chatham Cl DE56 ... 3 C2
Chatham St DE23 ... 36 C4
Chatsworth Cres
  DE22 .... 12 B3
Chatsworth Ct
  DE24 .... 45 C4
Chatsworth Dr DE3. 25 A3
Chatsworth St
  DE23 .... 27 A1
Chatteris Dr DE21... 13 C1
Chaucer Terr DE23 . 36 B3
Cheadle Cl DE23 ... 26 A1
Cheam Cl DE22 .... 16 A2
Cheapside
  2 Belper DE56 ...... 2 B1
  Derby DE1......... 60 B3
Chedworth Dr
  DE24 .... 39 C2
CHELLASTON 48 A1
Chellaston Inf Sch
  DE73 .... 48 A2
Chellaston Jun Sch
  DE73 .... 47 C1
Chellaston La DE72,
  DE73 .... 49 A1
Chellaston Park Ct
  DE73 .... 47 C1
Chellaston Rd DE24. 47 B4
Chellaston Sch
  DE73 .... 47 C1
Chelmarsh Cl DE73. 48 A3
Chelmorton Pl
  DE21 .... 20 B4
Chelmsford Cl DE3.. 24 B3
Chelsea Cl DE21 ... 16 B2
Chelwood Rd DE73 . 47 C2
Chequers La DE21.. 19 C2

Chequers Rd DE21.. 19 C1
Cheribough Rd
  DE74 .... 53 A1
Cheriton Gdns
  DE23 .... 34 A3
Cherrybrook Dr
  DE21 .... 15 A3
Cherry Cl DE3 ..... 25 C2
Cherrydale Ct DE23 34 C2
Cherry Tree Ave
  DE56 .... 3 A4
Cherry Tree Cl
  DE22 .... 26 A4
CHERRYTREE HILL 21 A1
Cherry Tree Hill Inf
  Sch DE21..........21 A1
Cherry Tree Hill Jun
  Sch DE21..........21 A1
Cherry Tree Mews
  DE21 .... 30 A4
Chertsey Rd DE3... 24 B2
Chesapeake Rd
  DE21 .... 21 A2
Cheshire St DE24 .. 38 A1
Chester Ave DE22... 9 C1
Chester Ct
  Derby, Little Chester
  DE21 .... 19 A4
  Derby, Spondon
  DE21 .... 31 A3
Chesterfield Rd
  DE56 .... 2 C2
Chesterford Ct
  DE23 .... 34 B2
Chester Green Rd
  DE1 .... 18 C3
Chesterton Ave
  DE23 .... 36 A3
Chesterton Rd
  DE21 .... 22 A2
Chestnut Ave
  Belper DE56 .... 4 B4
  Chellaston DE73....47 C3
  Derby DE1......... 24 C3
  Derby, Rose Hill
  DE23 .... 27 C2
  Holbrook DE56 ...... 5 A1
Chestnut Cl DE56 ... 7 B1
Chestnut Gr
  Borrowash DE72....32 B2
  Etwall DE65 .... 58 B2
Chevely Ct DE21.... 19 C4
Cheverton Cl DE24.. 39 C1
Chevin Alley DE56 ... 4 A1
Chevin Ave
  Borrowash DE72....32 B2
  Derby DE23........ 35 B2
Chevin Mews DE56.. 4 A4
Chevin Pl DE1 ..... 18 B3
Chevin Rd
  Belper, Milford
  DE56 .... 4 A2
  Derby DE1......... 18 B3
  Duffield DE56 .... 7 B4
Chevin Vale DE56... 7 B4
Chevin View DE56... 2 B2
Cheviot St DE22 ... 17 B1
Cheyenne Gdns
  DE21 .... 21 B1
Cheyne Wlk DE21... 17 B2
Chilson Dr DE3 .... 24 B3
Chime Cl DE21...... 14 A2
Chingford Ct DE22 . 17 A2
Chinley Rd DE21.... 14 C1
Chiswick Cl DE22 .. 16 B2

Christchurch Ct
DE1.............. **60** B4
Church Cl DE73... **48** A1
Churchdown Cl
DE21..............**15** A2
Church Dr DE56 ..... **7** C1
Church Hill
Derby DE21.......**30** C4
Etwall DE65 ....**58** B4
Churchill Cl DE72...**41** C2
Church La
■ Belper DE56 .... **2** B2
Breadsall DE21.......**14** A4
Castle Donington
DE74 ....**53** B1
Derby, Chaddesden
DE21 ....**20** C2
Derby, Darley Abbey
DE22..............**12** C2
Little Eaton DE21 ...**10** A3
Mackworth DE22 ...**16** B3
Church La N ■
DE22..............**12** B3
Church Mews
Derby DE21.......**30** C4
Melbourne DE73....**59** B2
Church Rd DE22 ..... **8** A1
Churchside Wlk
DE22..............**27** A4
Church Sq DE73...**59** B1
Church St
Belper DE56 .... **2** C1
Derby, Alvaston
DE24 ....**39** B3
Derby DE23........**26** B1
Derby, Rose Hill
DE23..............**27** C2
Derby, Spondon
DE21 ....**21** C1
Holbrook DE56.......**5** A1
Kilburn DE56........**6** A2
Melbourne DE73....**59** B2
Ockbrook DE72....**32** B4
Church View
Belper DE56 .... **2** C2
Breaston DE72 ......**41** C1
Duffield DE56 .... **7** B1
Church Wlk
■ Belper DE56 .... **2** B2
Derby DE22........**12** B4
Duffield DE56 .... **7** C1
CINDERHILL **5** C3
Circle The DE24...**36** A1
City Gate DE24...**28** C2
City Gate Bsns Pk
DE24 ....**28** C2
City Rd DE1........**18** C3
Clapgun St DE74...**53** B1
Clare Ho DE1......**61** B1
Clarence Rd DE23...**27** B1
Clarkes La DE72...**51** B3
Clarke St DE1......**60** C4
Clay St DE72.......**40** C1
Cleveland Ave
Derby DE21.......**21** A1
Draycott DE72 ......**40** C1
Clifford St DE24...**28** C2
Clifton Dr DE3.....**25** A3
Clifton Rd DE22...**11** C3
Clifton St DE1.....**61** D1
Clinton St DE21...**19** C2
Clipstone Gdns
DE21..............**15** A2

Cloisters Ct DE1...**14** B2
Close The
Derby, Allestree
DE22..............**12** B2
Derby, Normanton Park
DE23..............**26** C2
Cloudwood Cl
DE23..............**26** A1
Clovelly Ct DE22...**17** C4
Clover Cl DE21.....**22** B1
Cloverdale Dr DE24 **45** C2
Cloverslade DE65...**42** C1
Cluster Rd DE56 .... **2** B2
Clusters Ct ■ DE56.. **2** B2
Coach Dr DE22 ..... **8** B3
Cobden St DE22...**17** C1
Cobham Cl DE24...**45** A3
Cobthorn Dr DE22...**11** B3
Coburn Pl DE1......**60** A3
Cockayne St N
DE24..............**38** A2
Cockayne St S
DE24..............**38** A2
Cockcharme Gapp
DE74..............**53** B4
Cock Pitt The DE1...**60** C3
Cockshut Lane Bsns
Ctr DE73..........**59** A2
Cod Beck Cl DE24...**39** C2
Coke St DE22.......**17** C1
Coldstream Wlk
DE24..............**45** B4
Cole La DE72.......**32** C3
Coleman St DE24...**38** A3
Coleraine Cl DE21...**30** A4
Coleridge St
Derby, Littleover
DE23..............**36** A2
Derby, Normanton
DE23..............**36** B3
College Mews DE1...**18** A1
Collier La DE72.....**32** B4
Collingham Gdns
DE22..............**16** C1
Collis Cl DE24......**38** A3
Collumbell Ave
DE72..............**23** B1
Colombo St DE23...**28** A1
Coltsfoot Dr DE24...**45** C2
Columbine Cl DE21 **14** C1
Colvile St DE22.....**17** C2
Colwell Dr DE24....**39** C1
Colwyn Ave DE23...**26** C1
Colyear St DE1.....**61** B3
Comfrey Cl DE23...**34** B2
Commerce St
Derby DE24........**38** B4
Melbourne DE73....**59** A2
Common End DE65 .**58** B2
Common Piece La
DE65..............**43** B1
Common The DE22...**8** A4
Compton Ave DE72 .**51** A3
Compton Cl ■
DE24..............**39** B2
Coniston Ave DE21 **22** A2
Coniston Cres
DE21..............**13** C2
Connaught Rd
DE22..............**26** B4
Consett Cl DE21....**13** C1
Consort Gdns DE21.**15** B3
Constable Ave
DE23..............**26** B2
Constable Dr DE23..**26** B3
Constable La DE23..**26** B3
Conway Ave DE72...**32** C2
Cook Cl DE56.......**3** D3

Cookham Cl DE3....**24** B2
Cooks Dr DE74.....**53** A1
Co-operative St
DE23..............**27** B2
Coopers Cl DE72....**32** C1
Cooper St DE22....**17** C2
Copecastle Sq DE1 .**61** C2
Cope Ct DE24......**36** C1
Copeland St DE1 ...**61** C2
Copes Way DE21...**20** C4
Copperleaf Cl DE22 **61** A2
Coppice Cl
Derby DE22........**12** B1
Kilburn DE56........**6** B1
Coppice End Rd
DE22..............**11** B1
Coppicewood Dr
DE23..............**25** C1
Copse Gr DE23 .....**34** C3
Corbel Cl DE21 .....**14** A2
Corbridge Gr DE23..**34** C3
Corby Cl DE24 .....**38** B1
Cordelia Way DE73 .**47** B2
Corden Ave DE3 ....**25** C2
Corden St DE23.....**27** C2
Cordville Cl DE21...**21** A1
Cordwell Cl DE74...**52** C1
Corfe Cl DE23 ......**35** C2
Coriander Gdns
DE23..............**45** A4
Corinium Ct DE23...**39** C1
Cornflower Dr
DE21..............**15** A3
Cornhill Cl DE22 ...**12** B4
Cornhill Cl DE56....**7** A3
Cornmill Cl DE72 ...**39** C1
Corn Mkt DE1 ......**60** B3
Cornwall Rd DE21 ..**19** C2
Coronation Ave
Belper DE56 .... **2** C3
Derby DE24........**39** B1
Coronation Cl DE73 **59** B3
Coronation St DE23 **37** A4
Coronet Ct DE21....**15** C3
Corporation St DE1 **60** B3
Cotswold Cl DE23..**35** B4
Cottage Cl DE56.....**3** B1
Cottisford Cl DE23 .**34** C4
Cottonbrook Rd
DE23..............**37** A4
Cotton La DE24 .....**28** B1
Countess Gr DE73 ..**50** B4
Countisbury Dr
DE21..............**14** C2
Courtland Dr DE24..**39** A2
Courtland Gdns
DE24..............**39** A3
Courtland Rd DE65 .**58** C2
Courtney Way DE56..**3** C3
Court The DE24.....**39** A2
Courtway Cres
DE73..............**50** A4
Courtyard Mews
DE24..............**38** C2
Courtyard Pl DE21 ..**22** A1
Courtyard The DE56..**3** C1
Coverdale Wlk
DE24..............**39** B3
Covert The DE21....**31** A4
Cowdray Cl DE24...**39** A2
COWHILL..........**4** B4
Cowley St DE22....**18** A3
Cowper St DE24....**36** C1
Cowsley Rd DE21...**19** C3
Cowslip Mdw DE72 .**40** C1
Cox Green Cl DE23..**34** B3
Coxon St DE21.....**21** A1

Crabtree Cl
Castle Donington
DE74..............**56** A4
Derby DE22........**11** B4
Crabtree Hill DE22..**11** B3
Crab Tree Hill
DE21..............**10** A4
Craddock Ave DE21 **31** A3
Craiglee Ct ■
DE24..............**45** A3
Cranberry Gr DE23..**34** B2
Cranhill Cl DE23 ...**34** B2
Cranmer Rd DE21...**60** D3
Crawley Rd DE24 ...**38** B1
Crayford Rd DE24...**38** C1
Crecy Cl DE22 ......**26** B3
Crescent The
Breaston DE72 ......**41** B1
Derby, Boulton
DE24..............**38** A2
Derby, Chaddesden
DE21..............**20** B1
Cressbrook Way
DE21..............**15** A3
Cressida Ct DE73 ...**47** A2
Cresta Gr DE21.....**14** B1
Crest The DE22 .....**12** A2
Crewe St DE23......**27** B1
CREWTON.........**38** B4
Crewton Way DE24 .**38** B3
Crich Ave DE23 .....**26** B2
Crich Cir DE23......**26** B2
Cricketers Ct DE23..**35** C4
Cricklewood Rd
DE22..............**17** A2
Cringle Mews DE21 **14** A2
Croft Cl
Derby DE21........**22** B1
Ockbrook DE72......**32** B4
Croft End DE21.....**10** A4
Crofters Ct DE21...**14** A2
Croft La DE21......**13** C3
Croft The
Belper DE56 .... **5** A3
Derby DE23........**35** C4
■ Melbourne DE73..**59** A3
Cromarty Cl DE24...**45** B4
Cromer Cl DE3 .....**24** B1
Cromford Dr DE3 ...**24** A4
Cromford Rd DE21..**20** C4
Crompton St DE1...**61** B2
Cromwell Ave DE65 **43** A2
Cromwell Rd DE21..**27** B2
Cropton Cl DE24....**39** B2
Crosby St DE22.....**26** C4
Cross Cl DE23 ......**35** B4
Crossdale Gr DE21..**15** B3
Cross St DE22......**17** C2
Crownland Dr DE73 **48** A2
Crown Mews DE22..**27** A3
Crown St
Derby DE22........**27** A3
Duffield DE56 .... **7** B3
Crown Terr ■ DE56..**2** B2
Crown Way DE73 ...**50** B4
Crown Wlk DE1.....**61** B2
Crowshaw St DE24..**37** A4
Croydon Wlk DE21 .**31** A4
Crystal Cl DE3 .....**24** C4
Cuckmere Cl DE22...**9** C1
Culholme Rd DE21..**60** D3
Culworth Cl DE56....**3** C2
Culworth Ct DE21...**15** A2
Cumberland Ave
DE21..............**20** A2
Cumberland Cres
DE72..............**32** A2
Cumbria Wlk DE3...**24** B1
Cummings St DE23 .**27** C2

Curborough Dr
DE24..............**39** C2
Curlew Cl DE24.....**45** A4
Curzon CE Prim Sch
The DE22...........**8** B2
Curzon Cl DE22....**11** B4
Curzon Ct DE56.....**7** B2
Curzon La
Derby DE24........**38** C4
Duffield DE56 .... **7** A2
Curzon Rd DE21 ...**20** B3
Curzon St DE1.....**60** A3
Cut La DE1, DE21...**19** A3
Cutler Way DE3.....**24** C4
Cuttlebrook Cl
DE23..............**36** A2
Cypress Wlk DE21 ..**21** A1

D

Dahlia Dr DE21 .....**15** B3
Dairy House Rd
DE23..............**28** A1
Dakota Rd DE74....**56** B2
Dalbury Wlk DE23 ..**35** B1
Dale Cl DE72.......**41** C2
Dale Com Prim Sch
DE23..............**27** B1
Dale Ct DE56.......**6** A2
Dale Park Ave DE56..**6** B2
Dale Rd
Derby, Alvaston
DE24..............**39** A3
Derby DE21, DE72...**22** C2
Derby, Normanton
DE23..............**27** B2
Dalesgate Cl DE23 .**35** B1
Dale View Gdns
DE56..............**6** A2
Dalkeith Ave DE24..**38** B1
Dalness Ct ■ DE24 .**45** A3
Dalton Ave DE23....**26** B3
Dam Side DE56 .....**2** C2
Damson Gr DE24....**38** A4
Danebridge Cres
DE21..............**14** C1
Danesby Cres DE5...**6** B3
Danesby Rise DE5 ...**6** B3
Darby St DE23......**27** B2
Dark La DE56.......**4** C1
DARLEY ABBEY....**12** C2
Darley Abbey Dr
DE22..............**12** B2
Darley Gr DE1 .....**18** C3
Darley La DE1......**60** B4
Darley Park* DE22 ..**12** B2
Darley Park Dr
DE22..............**12** B1
Darley Park Ho
DE22..............**12** C1
Darley Park Rd
DE22..............**12** B1
Darley St DE22.....**12** C1
Darsway DE74......**52** C2
Dartford Pl DE24...**38** C1
Darwin Ave DE24...**47** A4
Darwin Pl DE1......**60** C3
Darwin Rd DE3.....**25** A3
Darwin Sq DE1 .....**61** B2
Dashwood St DE23..**61** B1
Datchet Cl DE23....**34** C4
Davenport Rd DE24 **37** B4
Daventry Cl DE3 ....**24** B3
David's Cl DE73.....**47** C1
Da Vinci Com Coll
DE21..............**14** A1
Davis Ho ■ DE1.....**61** B2
Dawlish Ct DE24....**39** B3

Dawsmere Cl DE21 . 13 C1
Daylesford Dr DE23 . 34 C4
Days La DE56 . . . . 2 B1
Dayton Cl DE21 . . . . . 21 B1
Dayton Ct DE22 . . . . . 18 A4
Deacon Cl DE21 . . . . 14 A2
Deadman's La DE24 28 C2
Dean Cl DE23 . . . . . . 25 C2
Dean Ct DE23 . . . . 27 A2
Deans Dr DE72 . . . . . 32 A2
Dean St DE23 . . . . 27 A3
Deborah Dr DE21 . . . 20 C3
Dee Cl DE24 . . . . 45 B3
Deepdale Ave DE72 . 32 B3
Deep Dale La DE24,
DE73 . . . . 45 C1
Deepdale Rd
Belper DE56 . . . . 3 A3
Derby DE21 . . . . 31 B3
Deer Park View
DE21 . . . . 22 B2
De Ferrers Ct DE56 . . 7 B2
Degge St DE1 . . . . . . 61 B2
Deincourt Cl DE22 . . 22 C2
Delamere Cl
Breaston DE72 . . . . . 41 C2
Derby DE21 . . . . 14 C1
Delven La DE74 . . . . . 53 B1
Denarth Ave DE24 . . 47 B3
Denbigh St DE21 . . . . 20 A3
DENBY BOTTLES 6 B3
Denison Gdns DE21 21 A2
Dennis Cl DE23 . . . . . 34 A3
Denstone Dr DE24 . . 48 A4
Dentdale Ct DE24 . . 39 B3
Denver Rd DE3 . . . . 24 C3
Depot St DE23 . . . . . . 27 C2
DERBY 60 C4
Derby Assembly
Rooms★ DE1 . . . . . 60 B3
Derby City General
Hospl DE22 . . . . . . 26 A2
Derby Coll DE22 . . . . 16 C1
Derby Gram Sch for
Boys DE23 . . . . 34 B3
Derby High Sch
DE23 . . . . 26 A1
Derby Industrial
Museum★ DE1 . . 60 B3
Derby La DE23 . . . . . 36 B4
Derby Moor Com
Sports Coll DE23 . . 35 A3
Derby Museum & Art
Gallery★ DE1 . . . . 60 B3
Derby Rd
Borrowash DE21,
DE72 . . . . 31 C2
Chellaston DE73 . . . . 47 C2
Derby, Spondon
DE21 . . . . 30 B3
Draycott DE72 . . . . . 40 A2
Etwall DE65 . . . . 58 A3
Kilburn DE56 . . . . 6 A3
Melbourne DE73 . . . . 59 A3
Derbyshire Cty Cricket
Gd DE21 . . . . 19 B2
Derbyshire Dr DE74 . 53 B2
Derbyshire Royal
Infmy DE1 . . . . 61 C1
Derby Small Bsns Ctr
Derby DE1 . . . . 61 C1
Derby, Pear Tree
DE23 . . . . 28 A1
Derby Sta DE1 . . . . 28 B4
Derby Trad Est
DE21 . . . . 19 A4

Derby Univ
(Mickleover Site)
DE3 . . . . 25 B3
Derrington Leys
DE24 . . . . 39 C2
Derventio Cl DE1 . . . 18 C3
Derwent Ave
Belper DE56 . . . . 4 B3
Borrowash DE72 . . . . 32 B3
Derby DE72 . . . . 12 C4
Derwent Bsns Ctr
DE1 . . . . 60 C4
Derwent Cl DE22 . . 12 C4
Derwent Com Sch
DE21 . . . . 19 B2
Derwent Ct DE56 . . . 3 A2
Derwent Dr DE24 . . 45 A2
Derwent Ho DE21 . . 19 B2
Derwent Par DE21,
DE24 . . . . 29 A3
Derwent Park Ho
DE22 . . . . 12 C1
Derwent Rd DE21 . . 30 C3
Derwent Rise DE21 . 31 B4
Derwentside Ind Pk
DE56 . . . . 4 A3
Derwent St
Belper DE56 . . . . 2 B1
Derby DE1 . . . . 60 C4
Draycott DE72 . . . . . 40 C1
Derwent Vale DE56 . . 4 A4
Derwent View
Belper, Milford
DE56 . . . . 4 B2
Belper, Mount Pleasant
DE56 . . . . 4 B2
Devas Gdns DE21 . . 21 C1
Devonshire Ave
Borrowash DE72 . . . 32 B2
Derby DE22 . . . . 12 B3
Devonshire Dr
Derby DE3 . . . . 25 A3
Duffield DE56 . . . . . . 7 A1
Devonshire Wlk
DE1 . . . . 61 C2
Dewchurch Dr
DE23 . . . . 36 A1
Dexter St DE23 . . . . . 28 B2
Diamond Dr DE21 . . . 14 B3
Dickens Sq DE23 . . . . 36 B3
Dickinson St DE24 . . 28 C2
Diseworth Cl DE73 . . 47 C2
Diseworth Rd DE74 . 56 A3
Dodburn Ct DE24 . . 45 A4
Doles La DE65 . . . . . . 43 A3
Dolphin Cl DE21 . . . . 22 C2
Domain Dr DE73 . . . . 47 B1
Donald Hawley Way
DE56 . . . . 7 C2
Donegal Wlk DE21 . . 29 C4
Donington Cl DE23 . 36 A1
Donington Dr DE23 . 36 A1
Donington Grand Prix
Collection Museum★
DE74 . . . . 55 A2
Donnington Park
Motor Racing Circuit
DE74 . . . . 54 C2
Dorchester Ave
DE21 . . . . 20 B3
Dorking Rd DE22 . . . 17 A2
Dorrien Ave DE23 . . 36 C3
Dorset St DE21 . . . . . 19 C2
Douglas St DE23 . . . . 28 A2
Dove Cl
Derby DE3 . . . . 25 C3
Kilburn DE56 . . . . 6 B2
Dovecote DE74 . . . . 53 B1

Dovecote Dr DE72 . . 32 A2
Dovedale Ave DE24 . 39 B3
Dovedale Cres DE56 . 3 A3
Dovedale Day Hospl
DE1 . . . . 61 C1
Dovedale Rd DE21 . . 31 B3
Dovedale Rise
DE22 . . . . 11 C1
Dovedales The DE3 . 24 C2
Dover Ct DE23 . . . . . . 27 C2
Dover St DE23 . . . . . . 27 C1
Doveridge Wlk
DE23 . . . . 35 B1
Dovestone Gdns
DE23 . . . . 26 A1
Dovewood Ct DE23 . 34 C3
Dower Cl DE22 . . . . . 12 C1
Downham Cl DE3 . . . 25 A1
Downing Cl DE22 . . 16 B2
Downing Ho DE22 . . 16 B2
Downing Rd DE21 . . 19 C1
Drage St DE1 . . . . . . 19 A3
DRAYCOTT 40 B1
Draycott Com Prim
Sch DE72 . . . . 40 C1
Draycott Dr DE3 . . . 24 B3
Draycott Mills
DE72 . . . . 40 C1
Draycott Rd
Borrowash DE72 . . . 32 B1
Breaston DE72 . . . . . 41 B1
Drayton Ave DE22 . . 16 B2
Dresden Cl DE3 . . . . 24 B2
Drewry Ct DE1 . . . . . 18 B1
Drewry La DE22 . . . . 27 B4
Dreyfus Cl DE21 . . . . 22 B1
Drummond Way
DE73 . . . . 47 B2
Drum The DE22 . . . . 12 B3
Drury Ave DE21 . . . . 30 C4
Dryden St DE23 . . . . . 36 B3
Drysdale Rd DE3 . . . 24 C3
Duchess Way DE73 . 50 A4
Duesbury Cl DE24 . . 38 A3
Duesbury Ct DE3 . . . 33 A3
Duesbury Pl DE3 . . . 33 A3
DUFFIELD 7 C2
Duffield Cl DE56 . . . . 7 C2
Duffield Rd DE22 . . . 9 B1
Duffield Sta DE56 . . 7 C3
Dukeries La DE21 . . 15 A2
Duke's Bldgs DE56 . . 4 B1
Duke St DE1 . . . . 60 B4
Duluth Ave DE21 . . . 20 C3
Dulverton Ave
DE24 . . . . 44 C2
Dulwich Rd DE22 . . 16 A2
Dunbar Cl DE24 . . . . 45 B3
Duncan Cl DE56 . . . . 3 A4
Duncan Rd DE23 . . . 36 B4
Dundas Way DE73 . . 47 B1
Dunedin Cl DE3 . . . . 25 A3
Dunkery Ct DE21 . . . 14 C2
Dunkirk DE21 . . . . . . 61 A2
Dunnicliffe La
DE73 . . . . 59 A2
Dunoon Cl DE24 . . . . 45 B3
Dunsmore Dr DE21 . 14 B2
Dunstall Park Rd
DE24 . . . . 37 C4
Dunton Cl DE21 . . . . 60 D3
Dunvegan Cl DE24 . 45 A2
Durham Ave DE21 . . 20 A2
Durley Cl DE24 . . . . 39 B3
Durward Cl DE24 . . . 37 B3

Eagle Cl DE56 . . . . . . 4 A4
Ealing Cl DE22 . . . . . 17 A2
Eardley Cl DE21 . . . . 21 A1
Earls Cres DE21 . . . . 15 A2
Earlswood Ct DE72 . 41 C2
Earlswood Dr DE3 . . 25 B4
East Ave DE3 . . . . 25 A3
Eastbrae Rd DE23 . . 35 C3
East Cl DE22 . . . . 12 A2
East Cres DE56 . . . . . . 5 A2
East Croft Ave
DE23 . . . . 35 C1
Eastgate DE21 . . . . 60 D4
East Lawn DE65 . . . . 43 A2
Eastleigh Dr DE3 . . . 25 A2
East Midlands Airport
DE74 . . . . 56 C2
East Midlands
International Airport
DE74 . . . . 56 C2
East Midlands Nuffield
Hospl DE23 . . . . . . 34 B2
East Service Rd
DE21 . . . . 30 A3
East St DE1 . . . . 61 B3
Eastway DE74 . . . . . 53 B1
Eastwood Ave DE23 . 26 B2
Eastwood Dr DE23 . 26 B2
Eaton Ave DE22 . . . . 9 C1
Eaton Cl DE22 . . . . . 9 B1
Eaton Ct
Derby DE1 . . . . 18 A2
Duffield DE56 . . . . . . 7 B1
Eaton Rd DE74 . . . . . 53 B1
Ecclesbourne Ave
DE56 . . . . 7 C2
Ecclesbourne Cl
DE56 . . . . 7 B2
Ecclesbourne Mdws
DE56 . . . . 7 B2
Ecclesbourne Sch The
DE56 . . . . 7 B2
Edale Ave
Derby, Alvaston
DE24 . . . . 39 A3
Derby DE23 . . . . 27 A2
Derby, Mickleover
DE3 . . . . 24 C2
Edale Cl DE22 . . . . . . 11 C1
Edale Dr DE21 . . . . . 31 B3
Edale Way DE56 . . . . 2 C3
Eden Rd DE21 . . . . . . 30 A4
Edensor Dr DE56 . . . 3 B4
Edensor Sq DE22 . . . 27 B4
Eden St DE24 . . . . . . 38 C4
Edgbaston Ct DE23 . 35 B4
Edge Hill DE73 . . . . . 47 C3
Edgelaw Ct 2
DE24 . . . . 45 A3
Edgware Rd DE22 . . 16 B2
Edinburgh Cres
DE24 . . . . 47 B3
Edith Wood Cl
DE24 . . . . 39 A1
Edmund Rd DE21 . . . 31 B3
Edmund's Sq DE3 . . . 33 A1
Ednaston Ave DE23 . 35 C1
Edward Ave DE21 . . 20 C1
Edwards Cres DE56 . . 6 B2
Edward St
Belper DE56 . . . . 2 C2
Derby DE1 . . . . 60 B4
Edwinstowe Rd
DE21 . . . . 15 A1
Eggesford Rd DE24 . 45 A2
Egginton Rd DE65 . . 58 B1

E

Egmanton Cl DE21 . . 15 A1
Eland Cl DE21 . . . . . . 22 C2
Eldon Ho 5 DE1 . . . . 61 B2
Eley Wlk DE1 . . . . . . 61 A1
Elgin Ave DE23 . . . . . 25 C1
Eliot Rd DE23 . . . . . . 35 A4
Elizabeth Cl DE21 . . 21 A1
Elkstone Cl DE21 . . . 15 A2
Ellastone Gdns
DE24 . . . . 39 A3
Ellendale Rd DE21 . . 21 A3
Ellesmere Ave
DE24 . . . . 28 C1
Ellison Ave DE72 . . . 51 A2
Elm Ave DE56 . . . . 4 C4
Elm Gr
Derby, Cherrytree Hill
DE21 . . . . 21 A1
Derby DE22 . . . . 8 B1
Elm Park Ct DE1 . . . 60 A5
Elms Ave DE23 . . . . . 26 A2
Elms Dr DE23 . . . . . . 26 A1
Elms Farm Way
DE23 . . . . 34 C4
Elms Gr DE65 . . . . . . 58 C2
Elms St DE1 . . . . 18 B3
Elm St DE72 . . . . 32 A2
Elmtree Ave DE24 . . 37 A3
Elm Tree Ave DE56 . . 6 C1
Elmwood Dr DE21 . . 13 C2
Elsecar Cl DE56 . . . . . 3 C3
Elton Rd DE24 . . . . . . 37 A4
Elvaston La DE24 . . 39 B3
Elvaston St DE72 . . . 41 A1
Embankment Cl
DE22 . . . . 16 B3
Emerald Cl DE21 . . . 14 C2
Emerson Sq DE23 . . 36 B2
Empress Rd DE23 . . . 61 A1
Endland Ind Est
DE1 . . . . 17 C1
Endsleigh Gdns
DE22 . . . . 16 B2
Enfield Rd DE22 . . . . 17 A2
Ennerdale Wlk
DE21 . . . . 13 C2
Ennis Cl DE21 . . . . . . 21 B3
Enoch Stone Dr
DE21 . . . . 30 A4
Enterprise Way
DE21 . . . . 60 C4
Epping Cl DE22 . . . . 16 A2
Epworth Dr DE24 . . 48 A4
Eskdale Wlk DE24 . . 39 C2
Essex St DE21 . . . . . . 19 C2
Eton St DE24 . . . . . . 29 A1
Etruria Gdns DE1 . . . 60 B5
Etta's Way DE65 . . . 58 B3
Ettrick Dr DE24 . . . . 45 B2
ETWALL 58 C2
Etwall Prim Sch
DE65 . . . . 58 B3
Etwall Rd DE3 . . . . . 24 B1
Etwall St DE22 . . . . . 18 A1
Euston Dr DE1 . . . . . 19 A3
Evans Ave DE22 . . . . 9 B1
Evanston Gdns
DE21 . . . . 21 A2
Evelyn Gr DE21 . . . . 20 C1
Evergreen Cl DE21 . . 14 C3
Evesham Cl DE21 . . 14 A1
Excelsior Ave DE24 . 38 B2
Exchange St DE1 . . . 60 B3
Exeter Ho DE1 . . . . . 60 C3
Exeter Pl DE1 . . . . . . 60 C3

Exeter St DE1......60 C4
Eyam Wlk DE56......2 C3
Eyes Ct DE56.........7 B2
Eyrie The DE24.....45 B3

F

Fairbourne Dr DE3..24 C4
Fairdene DE23......27 B2
Faires Cl DE72......32 C1
Faire St DE22.......27 A3
Fairfax Rd DE23....27 B2
Fairfield Ave DE72..32 B3
Fairfield Rd DE23...27 A1
Fairford Gdns DE23 34 C2
Fairisle Cl DE21.....15 B3
Fairlawns DE56......7 A2
Fairview Cl
  Derby DE23........34 C4
  Kilburn DE56.......6 C1
Fairview Grange
  DE56...............6 C1
Fairway Cl DE22....11 C2
Fairway Cres DE22..11 C2
Fairwood Dr DE24..39 C2
Falcons Rise DE56...3 B3
Falcon Way DE24...45 B2
Fallow Rd DE21.....22 B2
Falmouth Rd DE24..39 B1
Far Croft DE72......41 C2
Far La DE72.........23 C2
FAR LAUND...........3 B4
Far Laund DE56......3 A4
Farley Rd DE23.....26 C2
Farm Cl
  Belper DE56........3 B2
  Kilburn DE56.......6 B2
Farm Dr DE24......38 C1
Farmhouse Rd
  DE24..............45 B2
Farmlands La DE23.35 A2
Farm St DE22.......61 A1
Farnborough Gdns
  DE22..............13 A4
Farncombe La
  DE21..............14 B3
Farndale Ct DE21
  ....39 B2
Farneworth Rd DE3 24 C2
Farnham Cl DE3....24 B1
Farningham Cl
  DE21..............22 B1
Farnway DE22......12 A1
Farrier Gdns DE21..34 C3
Farringdon Cl DE22.16 B2
Faversham Cl DE24..38 B1
Fellow Lands Way
  DE73..............48 A2
Fellside
  Belper DE56........2 C2
  Derby DE21........22 B2
Fenchurch Wlk
  DE22..............17 A3
Fenton Rd DE3.....24 B2
Fenwick St DE24....37 C3
Fernhill Ct DE73....48 A3
Fernilee Gdns DE21.14 B1
Fernwood Cl DE23..35 B4
Ferrers Cl DE74.....53 A1
Ferrers Cres DE56....7 A2
Ferrers Way DE22...12 A2
Festival Ave DE72...41 B1
Field Cl DE72.......32 A3
Field Cres DE24.....38 C1
Field Ct DE56.........6 B1

Field Dr DE24........38 C1
Fieldfare Ct DE23...34 C2
Fieldgate Dr DE21..14 B2
Field Head Way
  DE21..............15 A3
Field La
  Belper DE56........2 B2
  Derby, Boulton
  DE24..............39 A1
  Derby, Chaddesden
  DE21..............20 C3
Field Rise DE23.....35 B3
Field Row **5** DE56..2 B2
Fieldsway Dr DE21..14 A2
Field View Cl DE24..39 A1
Fife St DE24.........38 B4
Filbert Wlk DE73....50 C4
Filey Wlk **4** DE21...13 C1
Fincham Cl DE21....13 C1
Finch Cres DE3.....33 B4
Finchley Ave DE22..16 B2
FINDERN.............43 A2
Findern Cl
  Belper DE56........3 A4
  Derby DE22........11 C1
Findern La DE65....42 B4
Findern St DE22....17 C1
Finmere Cl DE23....34 C4
Finningley Dr DE22 12 B2
Finsbury Ave DE22..17 A2
Finsley Wlk DE23...36 A2
Firs Cres DE22......12 A4
Firs Estate Prim Sch
  DE22..............27 A3
Firtree Gr DE21.....15 A2
Fisher La DE56.......7 B3
Fisher St DE24......38 A2
Fiskerton Way
  DE21..............15 A1
Five Lamps Ct DE1..18 B2
Five Lamps Ho DE1.60 A5
Flamstead Rd DE24.38 A2
Flat The DE56........6 A2
Fleet Cess DE56......2 B1
Fleet Pk DE56........2 C1
Fleet St DE23.......27 C2
Fleet The DE56......4 A4
Flint St DE24........37 C2
Flood St DE72......32 B4
Florence Ct DE1....61 D2
Folkestone Dr
  DE24..............38 C1
Folly Rd DE22.......13 A1
Ford La
  Breadsall DE21.....10 A1
  Derby DE22.........9 C1
Ford St
  Belper DE56........2 B2
  Derby DE1.........60 A4
Fordwells Cl DE23..34 C4
Fordyce Cl DE73....47 B1
Foremark Ave
  DE23..............36 A4
Forest Cl DE56......3 A3
Forester St DE1....61 B2
Forman St DE1,
  DE22..............60 A3
Forum Cl DE24.....39 C1
Fosbrook Dr DE74..52 C2
Fosse Cl DE72......32 B1
Foundry La DE56.....4 A2
Fountains Cl DE22..12 C4
Fowler Ave DE21....30 C4
Fowler St
  Derby DE22........18 A2
  Draycott DE72.....41 A1
Foxbrook Cl DE23..34 C4
Fox Cl DE24........45 A2

Foxdell Way DE73...48 A2
Foxes Wlk DE22.....12 A4
Foxfields Dr DE21..14 A2
Foxglove Cl DE21...14 C3
Foxlands Ave DE22..12 B2
Foxley Ct DE21......14 C2
Fox Rd DE74.......52 C2
Fox St DE1.........60 C4
Foyle Ave DE21.....29 C4
Frampton Gdns
  DE23..............34 B2
Franchise St DE22..27 A4
Francis St DE21.....19 C2
Franklyn Dr DE24...38 C2
Frazer Cl DE21......22 A2
Frederick Ave DE22.38 B2
Frederick St DE22..17 C2
Freehold St DE22...27 A4
Freeman Ave DE23..36 A2
Freesia Cl DE3......25 A1
Fremantle Rd DE21.25 A3
French St DE23.....27 A2
Fresco Dr DE21.....34 B3
Freshwater Ho
  DE24..............39 B3
Friar Gate DE1.....18 B1
Friar Gate Ct DE1..18 B1
Friar Gate House Sch
  DE1...............18 A2
Friars Cl DE22......12 C2
Friarsfield DE22....18 B4
Friary Ave DE24....38 A2
Friary St DE1.......60 A3
Fritchley Cl DE21...14 C1
Froggatt Cl DE22....9 B1
Frost Fields DE74...52 C1
Fulbrook Rd DE23..34 C4
Fulham Rd DE22....16 C1
Full St DE1.........60 B3
Fulmar Cl DE3......25 C3
Furrows Cl DE21...15 B3

G

Gable Ct DE3.......34 A4
Gainsborough Cl
  DE21..............15 A1
Gairloch Cl DE24...45 A2
Gala Dr DE24.......38 B3
Galway Ave DE21...30 A4
Garden Cres DE74..53 B1
Garden St DE1......60 A4
Garfield Ave DE72..40 C1
Garfield Cl DE23...35 B2
Garrick St DE24....38 C3
Garry Cl DE24......45 A2
Garsdale Cl DE24...39 C2
Garth Cres DE24...39 A2
Garthorpe Ct **4**
  DE21..............14 B2
Gary Cl DE23.......35 C1
Gascoigne Dr DE21.30 C4
Gaskell Ave DE23..36 A3
Gasny Ave DE74....53 B3
Gatcombe Cl DE21..15 A2
Gayton Ave DE23...35 C2
Gayton Com Jun Sch
  DE23..............35 C2
Gayton Thorpe Cl
  DE23..............34 B3
Gema Cl DE22......12 C4
George St
  Belper DE56........2 B2
  Derby DE1.........60 A3
  Melbourne DE73....59 A2
Georgina Ct DE74..53 B2
Gerard Cl DE21.....22 B2
Gerard Ct DE1.....61 A2

Gerard Gr DE65.....58 C3
Gerard St DE1......61 A2
Gertrude Rd
  Derby DE21........20 C4
  Draycott DE72.....40 C1
Ghyll Cl DE24......29 C1
Gibfield La DE56.....4 A4
Gilbert Cl DE21.....30 C4
Gilbert Cres DE56...7 B1
Gilbert St DE24....39 A2
Gilderdale Way
  DE21..............15 A3
Gillamoor Ct DE24.39 C2
Gilliver Gdns DE72.40 C1
Gisborne Cl DE3....25 A3
Gisborne Cres
  DE22..............12 B4
Gisborne Gn DE1...18 A2
Gladstone Cl DE73..47 C3
Gladstone Rd DE21.22 A1
Gladstone St DE21..27 A4
Glaisdale Nook
  DE24..............39 C2
Glamis Cl DE21.....15 A2
Glastonbury Rd
  DE24..............39 B3
Gleadsmoss La
  DE21..............14 C1
Glebe Rise DE23....26 C1
Glen Ave DE56......5 A1
Glencroft Dr DE24..45 A3
Glendale Dr DE21..22 B1
Glendevon Way
  DE73..............47 B2
Glendon Rd DE24..45 A3
Gleneagles Cl DE24.45 A3
Glenfield Cres DE3..24 B2
Glengarry Way
  DE24..............45 B4
Glenmore Dr DE24.45 A3
Glenmoy Cl DE23...35 C3
Glenorchy Ct DE21.15 A3
Glen Park Cl DE73..50 B4
Glen View DE56.....4 A4
Glenwood Rd DE73.50 C4
Glossop St DE24....37 A4
Gloster St DE24....29 A2
Glover Rd DE74....53 B2
Goathland Rd DE21.45 A2
Goldcrest Dr DE21..22 B2
Golders Green Wlk
  DE22..............16 C2
Gold La DE22.......16 A4
Goldstone Cl DE21..31 A4
Golf Cl DE23........25 C1
Golf La DE56.........7 B4
Goodale St DE23...27 C1
Goodrington Rd
  DE21..............15 B3
Goodsmoor Rd DE23,
  DE24..............36 A1
Goodsmoor Rd Ind Est
  DE24..............36 A1
Goods Rd DE56......4 A4
Goods Yd DE56......4 A3
Goodwood Dr DE24.39 B2
Gordon Rd
  Borrowash DE72...32 A1
  Derby DE23........27 B3
Gorse Cl DE23......35 A2
Gorsehill Gr DE23...34 C3
Gorsey Cl DE56......2 A4
Gorsty Leys DE65...43 A1
Gosforth Rd DE24..38 A4
Gower St DE1......61 B2
Grafham Cl DE73...48 A2
Grafton St DE23....27 A2

Grampian Prim Sch
  DE24..............45 A4
Grampian Way
  DE24..............45 B4
Grandstand Rd
  DE21..............19 B2
Grange Ave
  Breaston DE72.....41 C2
  Derby DE23........36 A3
Grange Cl DE73.....59 B3
Grange Dr DE74....53 A1
Grange Gate DE21..61 A1
Grangeover Way
  DE22..............26 C4
Grange Rd DE24....39 A2
Grange St DE23....28 A2
Grangewood Dr
  DE56..............4 B1
Grant Ave DE21....21 C4
Grantham Ave
  DE21..............14 A1
Granville Cl DE56....7 B2
Granville St DE1....18 A1
Grasmere Ave
  DE21..............22 A2
Grasmere Cres
  DE24..............45 B4
Grassthorpe Cl
  DE21..............15 A1
Gravel Pit La DE21..31 A4
Grayling St DE23...28 A2
Grays Cl DE74......53 B1
Great Northern Point
  DE21..............27 B4
Great Northern Rd
  DE1...............18 B1
Greatorex Ave
  DE24..............38 A1
Greenacres DE23...35 A4
Green Ave DE73....48 A1
Greenbank DE21...30 C4
Greenburn Cl DE23.35 B2
Greenfields Ave
  DE23..............35 A4
Greenfinch Cl DE21.22 B2
Green La
  Belper DE56........2 B2
  Burnaston DE65...42 A4
  Derby, Alvaston
  DE24..............39 B4
  Derby DE1.........61 B2
  Ockbrook DE72....23 B1
Greenland Ave
  DE22..............17 A1
Green Leas DE72...51 A3
Greenmount Cl
  DE23..............34 C2
Green Pk DE22.....16 C2
Greenside Cl DE3...24 B2
Green The
  Aston-on-T DE72...51 B3
  Belper DE56........2 C3
  Castle Donington
  DE74..............53 A1
  Derby DE22........11 C1
  Derby, Mickleover
  DE3...............24 C1
  Draycott DE72.....40 C1
  Findern DE65......43 A1
Greenville Croft
  DE73..............47 B1
Green Way DE65....43 A2
Greenway Cl DE72..32 A3
Greenway Dr DE23.25 C1
Greenway The
  DE72..............39 C1
Greenwich Dr N
  DE22..............17 B2

Greenwich Dr S
DE22 . . . . 17 A1
Greenwood Ave
DE21 . . . . 20 B4
Greenwood Cl
DE24 . . . . 37 C1
Greenwood Cl DE1 . 60 B4
Gregory Ave DE72 . . 41 B2
Gregorys Way DE56 . . 3 B3
Gregory Wlk DE23 . . 34 B2
Grendon Cl DE56 . . . 3 A4
Grenfell Ave DE23 . . 36 A2
Gresham Rd DE24 . . 37 B4
Grey St DE22 . . . . . . 61 A2
Griffe Field Prim Sch
DE23 . . . . 34 C2
Griffin Cl DE24 . . . . . 38 B3
Grimshaw Ave
DE24 . . . . 39 A3
Grindlow Rd DE21 . . 20 C4
Groombridge Cres
DE23 . . . . 34 C2
Grosvenor Dr DE23 . 34 C2
Grosvenor St DE24 . . 37 B4
Grovebury Dr DE23 . 35 B1
Grove Cl DE72 . . . . . 49 C4
Grove Ct DE72 . . . . . 49 C4
Grove Ho DE23 . . . . . 61 B1
Grove Pk DE65 . . . . . 58 B3
Groves Nook DE73 . 47 B1
Grove St DE23 . . . . . . 61 B1
Grove The DE3 . . . . 25 A2
Guildhall Theatre ★
DE1 . . . . 60 B3
Gurney Ave DE23 . . . 35 C2
Gypsy La DE72 . . . . . 40 A3

H

Haddon Cl DE22 . . . . 11 C3
Haddon Dr
Derby DE22 . . . . 11 C3
Derby, Mickleover
DE3 . . . . 25 A3
Derby, Spondon
DE21 . . . . 31 B4
Haddon St DE23 . . . . 27 A1
Haig St DE24 . . . . 38 B4
Hailsham Cl DE23 . . . 24 C3
Haines Cl DE24 . . . . 45 C4
Halifax Cl DE21 . . . . . 13 B1
Hallam Fields DE74 . . 56 B4
Hall Dyke DE21 . . . . . 21 C1
Hall Farm Cl DE1 . . . 61 B1
Hall Farm Rd DE56 . . 7 B1
Hallgate Cl DE21 . . . 15 B3
Hall Park Cl DE23 . . 26 A1
Hall St DE24 . . . . 38 C3
Halstock Dr DE24 . . 39 B4
Hambledon Dr
DE24 . . . . 45 A2
Hamblin Cres DE24 . . 45 C4
Hamilton Cl DE3 . . . . 25 B3
Hamilton Rd
Derby DE23 . . . . 27 B2
Derby, Spondon
DE21 . . . . 22 B2
Hamlet Ct DE73 . . . . . 47 B1
Hampden St DE23 . . 36 C4
Hampshire Rd
DE21 . . . . 19 B4
Hampstead Dr
DE22 . . . . 16 C2
Hampton Cl DE21 . . 22 B1
Hanbury Rd DE21 . . 20 B2
Handel St DE24 . . . . . 37 B4
Handford Ct DE22 . . 17 C2
Handford St DE22 . . 17 C1

Handyside St DE1 . . 60 B4
Hanger Bank DE72 . . 51 B3
Hanover Sq DE22 . . 16 C2
Hansard Gate DE21 . 60 D3
Hanslynn DE72 . . . . . 49 C4
Hanwell Way DE22 . 17 A2
Harcourt Pl DE74 . . 53 B2
Harcourt St DE1 . . . 61 B2
Hardacre Cl DE73 . . . 59 A3
Hardwick Ave DE22 . 11 C3
Hardwick Dr DE3 . . 25 A2
Hardwick Prim Sch
DE23 . . . . 27 C1
Hardwick St DE24 . . 37 B4
Harebell Cl DE21 . . . 14 C3
Harepit Cl DE24 . . . . 38 C1
Harewood Cl DE56 . . . 3 C3
Harewood Rd DE22 . 11 C3
Hargrave Rd DE72 . 23 B1
Hargreaves Cl
DE23 . . . . 34 C2
Harlech Cl DE21 . . . 22 C1
Harlesden Ave
DE22 . . . . 16 C3
Harlow Cl DE24 . . . . 47 C4
Harold Ct DE23 . . . . 28 A2
Harpswell Cl DE22 . 12 A2
Harpur Ave DE23 . . 35 A4
Harrier Rd DE56 . . . . 3 B3
Harrier Way DE24 . . 45 B3
Harriet St DE23 . . . 27 C3
Harriet Tubman Ho
DE23 . . . . 27 B1
Harringay Gdns
DE22 . . . . 17 B2
Harrington Ave
DE72 . . . . 32 B2
Harrington Rd
DE23 . . . . 26 B1
Harrington St
Derby, Allenton
DE24 . . . . 38 A2
Derby, Normanton
DE23 . . . . 36 C4
Draycott DE72 . . . . . 41 A1
Harrison St DE22 . . 27 A3
Harrogate Cres
DE21 . . . . 13 C1
Harrow St DE24 . . . . 29 A2
Hartington St DE1,
DE23 . . . . 61 B1
Hartington Way
DE3 . . . . 24 C2
Hartland Dr DE23 . . 36 A2
Hartshorne Rd
DE23 . . . . 35 B1
Harvest Way DE21 . . 15 B3
Harvey Rd
Castle Donington
DE74 . . . . 56 B4
Derby DE24 . . . . 38 A2
Hasgill Cl DE21 . . . . 15 B3
Haskeys Cl DE22 . . . 11 B2
Haslam's La DE21,
DE22 . . . . 13 A1
Haslemere Cl DE23 . 28 A2
Hassop Rd DE21 . . . 20 C4
Hastings St DE23 . . 27 C1
Hasting St DE74 . . . . 56 B4
Hatchmere Cl DE21 . 14 C1
Hatfield Rd DE24 . . 38 B1
Hathern Cl DE23 . . . 36 A1
Hathersage Ave
DE23 . . . . 36 A4
Hatton Cl DE73 . . . . 59 A2
Haulton Dr DE74 . . 53 A2
Havelock Rd DE23 . . 36 C4

Haven Baulk Ave
DE23 . . . . 34 A3
Haven Baulk La
DE23 . . . . 34 A3
Haven Ct DE24 . . . . 39 C2
Havenwood Gr
DE23 . . . . 35 B1
Hawke St DE22 . . . . 17 B1
Hawksdale Cl DE73 . 48 A2
Hawkshead Ave
DE21 . . . . 13 C1
Hawthorn Ave
DE24 . . . . 38 C3
Hawthorn Cres
DE65 . . . . 43 A2
Hawthorn Ct DE1 . . 60 A5
Hawthorne Ave
DE72 . . . . 32 B2
Hawthorne Cl DE56 . . 6 A4
Hawthorn Rd DE74 . . 53 B3
Hawthorn St DE24 . 37 B4
Hawthorns The
Belper DE56 . . . . 3 C3
Little Eaton DE21 . . . 10 B4
Hawtrey Gdns DE24 38 C3
Haycroft Cl DE23 . . 34 C3
Haydn Rd DE21 . . . . 20 B4
Haydock Park Rd
DE24 . . . . 38 A4
Hayes Ave
Breaston DE72 . . . . . 41 A1
Derby DE23 . . . . 35 C4
Hayes The DE65 . . . 42 C1
Hayfield Cl DE56 . . . . 3 A3
Hayfield Gdns DE23 35 A4
Hayford Pl DE24 . . . 26 C4
Haywood Cl DE24 . . 38 C1
Hazel Ave DE23 . . . . 35 C2
Hazel Cl DE65 . . . . 43 B2
Hazeldene Cl DE56 . 7 B4
Hazel Dr DE21 . . . . . 22 C2
Hazel Gr DE56 . . . . . 7 B2
Hazelrigg Cl DE74 . . 52 C2
Hazelwood Rd
Derby DE21 . . . . 20 B4
Duffield DE56 . . . . . . 7 A4
Headingley Ct DE23 . 35 B4
Heanor Ho DE21 . . . 31 A3
Heath Ave DE23 . . . . 26 B1
Heathcote Cl DE24 . 39 B1
Heath Ct DE24 . . . . . 45 B3
Heather Cl DE24 . . . 45 A3
Heather Cres DE23 . 35 B2
Heathermead Pl 2
DE21 . . . . 14 B1
Hebden Cl DE23 . . . 34 B2
Hebrides Cl DE24 . . 45 A3
Hedgebank Ct
DE21 . . . . 15 B3
Hedgerow Gdns
DE21 . . . . 15 B3
Hedgevale Cl DE23 . 34 C3
Hedingham Way
DE3 . . . . 33 C4
Heigham Cl DE24 . . 47 A3
Helston Cl DE24 . . . . 39 A2
Hemington Ct DE74 53 C3
Hemington Hill
DE74 . . . . 53 C2
Hemlock Cl DE21 . . 14 C3
Hendon Way DE22 . . 17 A2
Henley Gn DE22 . . . 16 B2
Henry St DE1 . . . . . . 60 A4
Herald Gr DE73 . . . 50 A4
Herbert Strutt Prim
Sch DE56 . . . . 4 A4
Hereford Rd DE21 . . 19 C4
Heritage Ct 4 DE56 . 2 B1

Hermitage Ave
DE72 . . . . 32 B2
Hermitage Ct DE21 . 15 A1
Heronswood Dr
DE21 . . . . 21 C2
Heron Way DE3 . . . 25 C2
Hexham Wlk DE21 . . 14 A1
Heydon Cl DE56 . . . 3 A4
Heyworth St DE22 . 17 C2
Hickling Cl DE24 . . . 47 A3
Highbury Cl DE21 . . 16 B2
High Edge Mews
DE56 . . . . 2 C3
Highfield Cotts
DE21 . . . . 20 A1
Highfield Gdns
DE22 . . . . 18 B3
Highfield La DE21 . . 20 B1
Highfield Mews
DE21 . . . . 20 A1
Highfield Rd
Belper DE56 . . . . 4 A4
Derby DE22 . . . . 18 B3
Derby, Littleover
DE23 . . . . 35 B3
Kilburn DE56 . . . . 6 A2
Little Eaton DE21 . . . 10 A4
Highfields Park Dr
DE22 . . . . 12 A1
Highgate Gn DE22 . . 16 C1
Highgates DE1 . . . . 61 B2
High Gr DE56 . . . . . . 3 C2
Highgrove Dr DE73 . 47 C2
High Pavement
DE56 . . . . 2 C1
High St
Belper DE56 . . . . 2 C2
Castle Donington
DE74 . . . . 56 A4
Chellaston DE73 . . . 48 A1
Kilburn DE56 . . . . 6 B2
Melbourne DE73 . . . 59 A2
Highwood Ave DE56 . 5 A3
High Wood Bank
DE56 . . . . 5 A3
Hilary Cl DE56 . . . . . 3 D3
Hilderstone Cl
DE24 . . . . 39 C2
Hill Brow DE1 . . . . . 61 B2
Hill Cl DE21 . . . . . . 31 A4
Hillcrest
Aston-on-T DE72 . . . 51 A4
Belper DE56 . . . . 3 D2
Hillcrest Dr DE56 . . . 6 B2
Hillcreste Dr DE73 . 47 C3
Hill Crest Rd DE21 . . 19 C3
Hillcroft Dr DE72 . . 32 B4
Hillside
Castle Donington
DE74 . . . . 53 B2
Findern DE65 . . . . . . 42 C2
Hillside Ave DE21 . . 20 C1
Hillside Cres DE21 . 31 B4
Hillside Rd DE21 . . . 31 B4
Hillside Rise DE56 . . 4 A4
Hill Sq The DE21 . . . 31 C4
Hills Rd DE72 . . . . . 41 B1
Hillsway
Chellaston DE73 . . . 47 C3
Derby DE23 . . . . 26 A1
Hill The DE22 . . . . . . 12 C1

Gre–Hom 69

Hill Top
Castle Donington
DE74 . . . . 56 A3
Derby DE21 . . . . 14 A3
Hilltop La DE56 . . . . 5 C4
Hill View DE56 . . . . . 7 A2
Hill View Cl DE7 . . . 6 C1
Hill View Gr DE21 . . 22 A1
Hillview Ho 1 DE1 . 61 B2
Hilton Cl DE3 . . . . . 24 C1
Hilton Gdns DE22 . 51 A2
Hilton Rd DE65 . . . . 58 B3
Hind Ave DE72 . . . . 41 B2
Hindscarth Cres
DE3 . . . . 25 A1
Hobart Cl DE23 . . . . 35 B2
Hobkirk Dr DE24 . . 45 B2
Hobson Dr DE21 . . . 31 B2
Hodge Beck Cl
DE24 . . . . 39 B2
Hodthorpe Cl DE21 . 15 A1
Holborn Dr DE22 . . 16 C3
Holbrook CE Prim Sch
DE56 . . . . 5 A1
HOLBROOK MOOR . 5 B1
Holbrook Rd
Belper DE56 . . . . 4 A4
Derby DE24 . . . . 39 A4
Holbrook View DE56 . 6 B2
Holcombe St DE23 . 28 A1
Holden Ave DE72 . . 51 A3
Holden Cl DE24 . . . . 38 C4
Holderness Cl DE24 45 A2
Hollies Rd DE22 . . . 11 C3
Hollington Cl DE21 . 20 A3
Hollis St DE24 . . . . . 38 C4
Holloway Rd
Derby DE24 . . . . 38 B2
Duffield DE56 . . . . . . 7 B3
Hollowood Ave
DE23 . . . . 35 B4
Hollow The
Castle Donington
DE74 . . . . 53 B2
Derby, Littleover
DE23 . . . . 35 B4
Derby, Mickleover
DE3 . . . . 33 C4
Hollybrook Way
DE23 . . . . 34 B2
Holly Brook Way
DE23 . . . . 34 B2
Holly Cl DE72 . . . . . 40 C1
Holly Ct
Aston-on-T DE72 . . . 51 A2
Derby DE3 . . . . 24 C1
Hollymoor Dr DE73 . 47 C2
Holm Ave DE21 . . . . 9 C3
Holme La DE21 . . . . 30 B3
Holmesfield Dr DE25 . 22 B2
Holmes Rd DE72 . . . 41 C2
Holmes St DE23 . . . 27 C2
Holmfield DE23 . . . . 36 A3
Holmleigh Way
DE73 . . . . 50 B4
Holmoak Cl DE21 . . 15 A3
Holt Ave DE24 . . . . . 39 B2
Holtlands Dr DE24 . 38 B1
Holyhead Dr DE21 . 15 A3
Holyrood Cl DE21 . . 22 C1
Holyrood Ho DE24 . 28 C1
Home Farm Cl
DE72 . . . . 23 B1
Home Farm Dr
DE22 . . . . 12 C4

Homefields Prim Sch
DE73 . . . . **47** B1
Honeycroft Cl DE56 . . **4** C4
Hope Ave DE3 . . . . . **24** C2
Hope St
Derby DE1 . . . . **61** C2
Melbourne DE73 . . . . . . **59** A2
Hopetoun St DE23 . . **36** C4
Hopping Hill DE56 . . . **4** A2
Hopping Hill Terr E
DE56 . . . . **4** B1
Hopping Hill Terr W
DE56 . . . . **4** B1
Hopton Cl DE21 . . . . **14** C1
Hopwell Rd DE72 . . . . **40** C4
Horeston Cotts DE7 . . **6** C1
Hornbeam Cl DE21 . . . **14** A2
Horncastle Rd
DE21 . . . . **13** C1
Hornsea Rd DE21 . . . . **13** C1
Horsley Cres DE56 . . . **5** A1
Horton St DE23 . . . . . **28** B2
Horwood Ave DE23 . . **26** C2
Hospital La DE3 . . . . **33** A3
Houghton Ct **7**
DE21 . . . . **14** B2
Hoult St DE22 . . . . . . **26** C4
Hounslow Rd DE22 . . **17** A2
Houston Cl DE21 . . . . **21** A2
Hoveton Cl DE24 . . . . **47** A3
Howard St DE22 . . . . **27** B2
Howden Cl DE3 . . . . . **24** B1
Howe St DE22 . . . . . . **17** C1
Howth Cl DE21 . . . . . **29** C4
Hoylake Cl DE3 . . . . **24** B3
Hoylake Dr DE3 . . . . **24** B3
Hoyland Ct DE56 . . . . **3** D3
Hubert Shaw Cl
DE24 . . . . **47** B4
Hucklow Ct DE21 . . . **15** A3
Hudson Way DE24 . . **28** B3
Hulland St DE1 . . . . . **61** D1
Hulland View DE21 . . **11** C1
Humber Cl DE24 . . . . **39** B2
Humbleton Dr
DE22 . . . . **16** C1
Hunter Dr DE56 . . . . . **6** A2
Hunter Rd DE56 . . . . . **3** C3
Hunters Croft DE24 . **45** B2
Huntingdon Ct
DE73 . . . . **59** B3
Huntingdon Dr
DE74 . . . . **53** A2
Huntingdon Gn
DE21 . . . . **19** B2
Huntley Ave DE21 . . **22** B1
Hutton St DE24 . . . . . **38** A2
Huxley Cl DE23 . . . . . **36** B3
Hyde Park Rd DE22 . **16** C2

I

Ibsley Cl DE24 . . . . . . **39** B2
Ilford Rd DE22 . . . . . **16** C1
Ilford Wlk DE22 . . . . **16** C1
Imperial Ct DE22 . . . . **8** B1
Industrial St **3**
DE23 . . . . **27** C2
Ingham Dr DE3 . . . . **33** C4
Ingleby Ave DE23 . . . **36** B3
Ingle Cl DE21 . . . . . . **22** A1
Ingledew Cl **1**
DE21 . . . . **14** B1
Inglewood Ave DE3 . **24** C4
Ingliston Cl DE24 . . . **39** C2

Instow Dr DE23 . . . . . **35** C2
Inveraray Cl DE24 . . **45** A3
Invernia Cl DE23 . . . . **36** A1
Iona Cl DE24 . . . . **45** B4
Ireton Cl DE56 . . . . . . **3** D1
Iron Gate DE1 . . . . . . **60** B3
Irvine Cl DE24 . . . . . **45** A3
Irving Pl DE24 . . . . . . **38** B3
Islay Rd DE24 . . . . . . **45** B4
Isleworth Dr DE22 . . **16** B2
ISLEY WALTON **55** A1
Ismay Rd DE21 . . . . . **20** B2
Ivybridge Cl DE21 . . **15** B3
Ivy Ct DE3 . . . . **24** C1
Ivy House Sch DE23 **28** B2
Ivyleaf Way DE21 . . **35** A2
Ivy Sq DE23 . . . . **28** B2

J

Jackdaw Cl DE22 . . . **17** C1
Jacksdale Cl DE22 . . **11** C1
Jackson Ave DE3 . . . **25** C2
Jacksons La DE65 . . **58** C1
Jackson St DE22 . . . . **27** A4
James Cl DE1 . . . . . . **18** A1
Jardine Ct DE72 . . . . **41** A1
Jarvey's La DE22 . . . **16** A4
Jarvis Ct DE24 . . . . . **45** B2
Jarvis Rd DE24 . . . . . **45** B2
Jasmine Cl DE21 . . . . **21** A1
Jawbone La DE73 . . . **59** C3
Jay Ct DE22 . . . . **17** C1
Jedburgh Cl DE24 . . **45** B2
Jefferson Pl DE24 . . . **38** B3
Jemison Cl DE23 . . . . **34** A3
Jenny's Ct DE56 . . . . . **3** B3
Jesop Dr DE24 . . . . . **45** B2
Jodrell Ave DE56 . . . . **3** C1
John Berrysford Cl
DE21 . . . . **20** B1
John F Kennedy Gdns
DE21 . . . . **21** B2
John Flamsteed Com
Sch DE56 . . . . **6** C4
John Lombe Dr
DE1 . . . . **18** C3
John O'Gaunts Way
DE56 . . . . **3** C2
John Port Cl DE65 . . **58** C3
John Port Sch
DE65 . . . . **58** B3
Johnson Ave DE24 . . **38** A3
John St DE1 . . . . **61** C2
Joseph St
Belper DE56 . . . . **2** B1
Derby DE23 . . . . **27** C1
Joseph Wright Ctr
(Derby Coll) The
DE1 . . . . **60** A4
Joseph Wright Terr
DE1 . . . . **60** B4
Jubalton Cl DE24 . . . **38** A2
Jubilee Bsns Pk
DE21 . . . . **60** C4
Jubilee Cl DE73 . . . . . **59** B2
Jubilee Ct DE56 . . . . . **4** B4
Jubilee Parkway
DE21 . . . . **60** C4
Jubilee Rd DE24 . . . . **47** C4
Junction St DE1 . . . . . **27** A4
Jury St DE1 . . . . **60** A3

K

Katrine Wlk DE24 . . . **36** A1
Kean Pl DE24 . . . . . . **38** B3
Keats Ave DE23 . . . . . **25** C1

Keble Cl DE1 . . . . **61** C1
Kedleston st DE1 . . . . **60** A4
Kedleston Cl DE22 . . **11** C1
Kedleston Ct **3**
DE22 . . . . **11** C2
Kedleston Gdns
DE1 . . . . **60** A4
Kedleston Old Rd
DE22 . . . . **17** C4
Kedleston Rd DE22 . **18** A3
Kedleston St DE1 . . . **60** A4
Kegworth Ave DE23 . **35** B2
Keldholme La DE24 . **39** C2
Kelmoor Rd DE24 . . . **39** A3
Kelso Wlk DE24 . . . . **45** B2
Kelvedon Dr DE23 . . **34** C2
Kemble Pl DE24 . . . . **38** B3
Kempton Park Rd
DE24 . . . . **37** C4
Kendal Wlk **1**
DE21 . . . . **13** C1
Kendon Ave DE23 . . . **36** A2
Kendray Cl DE56 . . . . . **3** C3
Kenilworth Ave
DE23 . . . . **36** B4
Kennedy Cl DE21 . . . **20** C3
Kensal Rise DE22 . . . **17** A2
Kensington St DE1 . . **61** A3
Kentish Ct DE1 . . . . . **19** A3
Kent St DE21 . . . . . . **19** C3
Kernel Cl DE23 . . . . **34** C4
Kerry St DE21 . . . . . . **19** C3
Kerry's Yd DE56 . . . . . **6** A2
Kershope Dr DE21 . . **15** A3
Kestrel Cl DE3 . . . . . **33** A3
Kestrel Ho DE24 . . . . **45** B2
Kestrels Croft DE23 . **45** B3
Keswick Ave DE3 . . . **36** A2
Kettlewell Cl DE24 . . **38** A2
Kevin Cl DE21 . . . . . **21** A4
Kew Gdns DE22 . . . . **17** A1
Keyhaven Cl DE21 . . **19** C4
Keynsham Cl DE24 . . **38** A4
Keys St DE1 . . . . **60** C4
Kibworth Cl DE21 . . . **21** A4
Kilbourne Rd DE56 . . . **3** B2
KILBURN **6** B2
Kilburn Inf Sch DE56 **6** A2
Kilburn Jun Sch
DE56 . . . . **6** B2
Kilburn La DE56 . . . . . **3** D1
Kilburn Toll Bar
DE56 . . . . **6** A3
Kildare Rd DE21 . . . . **30** A4
Kildrummy Cl DE73 . **47** B1
Killingworth Ave
DE24 . . . . **45** C4
Killis La
Belper DE56 . . . . **5** B3
Holbrook DE56 . . . . **5** B2
Kiln Croft DE65 . . . . **58** C3
Kilnsey Ct DE23 . . . . **34** B2
Kimberley Rd DE72 . **32** A2
Kinder Wlk DE22 . . . **27** A4
King Alfred St
DE22 . . . . **61** A2
Kingfisher Cl DE3 . . **33** A3
Kingfisher Wlk
DE24 . . . . **45** B2
Kingsbury Rd DE22 . **16** C2
Kingsclere Ave
DE21 . . . . **15** A2
Kings Croft DE22 . . . **12** B4
Kings Ct DE1 . . . . . . **60** B4
Kingsdale Gr DE73 . . **50** B4
Kings Dr DE3, DE23 . **26** A2
Kingsland Cl DE21 . . **14** B2
Kingsley Rd DE22 . . **11** C4

Kingsley St DE24 . . . **36** B1
Kingsmead Cl DE1 . . **60** A4
King's Mead Ho **1**
DE22 . . . . **18** B3
Kingsmead Ind Est
DE22 . . . . **17** C2
King's Mead Wlk
DE1 . . . . **60** A4
Kingsmuir Rd DE3 . . **24** B3
KING'S NEWTON . . . **59** B4
King St
Belper DE56 . . . . **2** B1
Derby DE1 . . . . **60** B4
Duffield DE56 . . . . **7** B3
Kingston St DE1 . . . . **18** B3
Kingsway DE22 . . . . . **17** A1
Kingsway Cres DE56 . **6** B2
Kingsway Hospl
DE3 . . . . **26** A4
Kingsway Ind Pk
DE22 . . . . **17** B1
Kingsway Park Cl
DE22 . . . . **17** B1
Kingsway Ret Pk
DE22 . . . . **17** B1
Kingswood Ave DE56 **3** B4
Kingswood Pl DE23 **26** A2
Kinross Ave DE21 . . . **19** B4
Kintyre Dr DE21 . . . . **19** B4
Kipling Dr DE3 . . . . . **24** C1
Kirk Dale Ave DE21 . **31** B3
Kirkfield Dr DE72 . . . **41** C2
Kirkistown Cl DE24 . **39** B2
Kirkland Cl DE74 . . . **53** A1
Kirkland Way **12**
DE24 . . . . **45** A3
Kirk Leys Ave N
DE21 . . . . **31** A4
Kirk Leys Ave S
DE21 . . . . **31** A4
Kirk's La DE56 . . . . . . **3** A1
Kirk St DE1 . . . . **19** A4
Kirkstead Cl DE21 . . **15** A1
Kitchener Ave DE23 . **36** B3
Kiwi Dr DE24 . . . . . . **38** B3
Knightsbridge
DE22 . . . . **16** C2
Knights Cl DE24 . . . . **45** B2
Knights Rd DE73 . . . **50** A4
Knoll Cl DE23 . . . . . **34** C4
Knowl Ave DE56 . . . . **2** A3
Knutsford Gn DE21 . . **13** C2
Kyle Gr DE21 . . . . . . **15** A3
Kynance Cl DE24 . . . **39** B1

L

Laburnum Cres
DE22 . . . . **11** C4
Laburnum Gr DE22 . **17** A1
Laburnum Way
DE65 . . . . **58** C2
Ladbroke Gdns
DE22 . . . . **16** B2
Ladybank Rd DE3 . . **24** B1
Ladybower Rd
DE21 . . . . **31** B4
Ladycroft Paddock
DE22 . . . . **12** A4
Ladygrove Cotts
DE23 . . . . **28** A3
Lady Mantle Cl
DE73 . . . . **47** B2
Ladysmith Rd DE72 . **32** A2
Ladywell Ct DE56 . . . **2** C1
Ladywood Ave DE56 . **3** A3
Lake Dr DE23 . . . . . . **36** B4

Lakeside Com Prim
Sch DE24 . . . . **29** A2
Lakeside Dr DE23 . . **34** C3
Lambe Ct DE23 . . . . **61** C1
Lambley Dr DE22 . . . **11** B2
Lambourn Ct DE22 . . **12** C3
Lambourn Dr DE22 . **13** A4
Lambrook Cl DE3 . . . **24** B2
Lampad Cl **4** DE73 . **59** A3
Lampeter Cl DE21 . . **15** A2
Lanark St DE21 . . . . **20** A3
Lancaster Rise DE56 . **2** C4
Lancaster Sports Ctr
DE1 . . . . **60** B4
Lancaster Wlk
DE21 . . . . **22** C2
Landau Forte Coll
DE1 . . . . **60** C4
Lander La DE56 . . . . . **2** C2
Landmere DE24 . . . . **45** B3
Langdale Dr DE21 . . **13** C1
Langford Rd DE3 . . . **24** C3
Langley Rd DE21 . . . **31** A3
Langley St DE22 . . . . **17** C2
Lang Rd DE24 . . . . . . **38** B2
Langsett Dr DE73 . . **48** A2
Langton The **4**
DE22 . . . . **18** A1
Lanscombe Park Rd
DE22 . . . . **12** A1
Lansdowne Ave
DE24 . . . . **38** B1
Lansing Gdns DE21 . **21** A2
Lantern Gr DE21 . . . . **24** C4
Lapwing Cl DE24 . . . **45** B2
Larch Cl DE22 . . . . . **11** C3
Larch Rd DE56 . . . . . . **6** C1
Larges St DE1 . . . . . **18** A1
Lark Cl DE23 . . . . . . **35** B2
Lark Hill DE3 . . . . . . **33** A3
Larkhill Cres DE24 . **45** C4
Larkin Cl DE24 . . . . **36** C1
Larkspur Cl DE21 . . **14** C3
Lashley Gdns DE21 . **14** B2
Lathbury Cl DE21 . . **13** C1
Lathkill Ave DE24 . . **39** B3
Lathkill Rd DE21 . . . **20** B4
Latimer Cl DE23 . . . **34** A3
Latimer St DE24 . . . . **37** C2
Latrigg Cl DE3 . . . . . **25** A1
Lauder Cl DE24 . . . . **45** B2
Launceston Rd
DE24 . . . . **39** A1
Laund Ave DE56 . . . . **3** A4
Laund Cl DE56 . . . . . **2** C4
Laund Farm DE56 . . . **3** B4
Laund Farm Mews
DE56 . . . . **3** B4
Laund Hill DE56 . . . . **2** C3
Laund Nook DE56 . . . **2** C3
Laurel Dr DE72 . . . . **51** A2
Laurie Pl DE24 . . . . . **38** C2
Lavender Row
DE22 . . . . **12** B1
Laverstoke Ct DE22 . **27** A4
Lawn Ave
Derby DE22 . . . . **11** C2
Etwall DE65 . . . . **58** C4
Lawn Heads Ave
DE23 . . . . **26** B2
Lawnlea Cl DE23 . . . **36** A1
Lawn Prim Sch
DE22 . . . . **11** C1
Lawnside DE21 . . . . **22** B1
Lawns The DE72 . . . . **51** B3
Lawnswood Cl
DE23 . . . . **35** B3

Lawrence Ave
Breaston DE72 . . . . **41** C2
Derby DE21. . . . . **21** A3
Lawrence St DE23 . . **36** B4
Lea Cl DE22 . . . . **12** A3
Leacroft Rd DE23 . . **28** A1
Lea Dr
Derby, Chaddesden
DE21 . . . . **20** B2
Derby, Mickleover
DE3 . . . . **25** A3
Leafenden Cl DE22 . . **12** C3
Leafgreen La DE23 . . **35** B2
Leake St DE22 . . . . . . **17** C1
Leamington Cl
DE23 . . . . **26** C1
Leander Cl DE23 . . . . **35** C3
Leaper St DE1 . . . . . . **18** A2
Leawood Gdns
DE21 . . . . **15** A3
Leche Croft DE56 . . . **3** C2
Ledbury Chase
DE24 . . . . **45** A2
Ledbury Pl **2** DE21 . **13** C1
Leeds Pl DE1 . . . . . . **61** D2
Lee Farm Cl DE73 . . **47** C1
Lees Brook Com
Sports Coll DE21 . . **21** A4
Lees Brook Ho
DE21 . . . . **20** C3
Leeside DE24 . . . . . . **29** C1
Lees The DE72 . . . . . . **39** C1
Leeway DE21 . . . . . . **30** C4
Leicester St DE22 . . **27** A3
Leighton Way **6**
DE56 . . . . **2** B1
Leman St DE22 . . . . . . **27** A3
Lens Rd DE21 . . . . . . **11** B2
Lenton Ave DE21 . . . **20** B2
Leominster Dr
DE21 . . . . **15** A2
Leonard Cl DE23 . . . . **61** B1
Leonard St DE1 . . . . . **61** C1
Leonard Wlk DE23 . . **61** B1
Leopold St DE1 . . . . **61** B2
Leslie Cl DE23 . . . . . . **34** A4
Leven Cl DE24 . . . . . . **45** C2
Leveret Cl DE73 . . . . **48** B2
Lewis St DE23 . . . . . . **27** B1
Lewiston Rd DE21 . . **21** A1
Lexington Rd DE21 . . **21** B2
Leycote Way DE56 . . **2** B3
Leyland Ct DE1 . . . . . **18** A3
Leyland Gdns DE1 . . **18** A3
Leylands DE22 . . . . . . **18** A4
Leyland St DE1 . . . . . **18** A3
Leys Ct DE56 . . . . **3** C2
Leys Field Gdns
DE73 . . . . **48** A2
Leytonstone Dr
DE22 . . . . **16** C1
Lichfield Dr DE24 . . **38** C3
Lidgate Cl DE3 . . . . . **24** B1
Liffey Ho DE24 . . . . . **38** A1
Lilac Ave DE24 . . . . . **16** C1
Lilac Cl DE24 . . . . . . **38** C2
Lilac Ct DE24 . . . . . . **38** C2
Lilac Way DE22 . . . . **11** C2
Lilian Prime Cl
DE24 . . . . **39** A4
Lilley St DE24 . . . . . . **39** A2
LILYPOOL **59** B2
Lilypools The DE73 . . **59** C2
Lime Ave
Derby, Breadsall
Hilltop DE21 . . . . . . **13** C2
Derby DE1 . . . . **61** A1
Duffield DE56 . . . . . . **7** B4

Lime Cres DE56 . . . . . . **4** C4
Lime Croft DE22 . . . . **12** B4
Limedale Ave DE21 . . **15** A3
Lime Gate Mews
DE23 . . . . **26** C2
Lime Gr
Derby DE21 . . . . **21** A1
Draycott DE72 . . . . . . **40** B1
Lime La DE21 . . . . . . **15** B3
Limerick Rd DE21 . . **30** A4
Limes Ave DE23 . . . . **24** C1
Limes Ct **3** DE3 . . . **24** C1
Lime Wlk DE23 . . . . **26** C1
Linacres Dr DE73 . . **48** A2
Lincoln Ave DE24 . . **38** C4
Lincoln Gn DE73 . . . **47** C2
Lindale Way DE73 . . **48** A2
Linden Cl DE56 . . . . . **6** C2
Lindford Cl DE21 . . . **14** B3
Lindisfarne Cl **4**
DE24 . . . . **45** A3
Lindon Dr DE24 . . . . **39** B2
Lindrick Cl DE3 . . . . **25** B1
Lindsey Cl DE21 . . . . **20** A2
Lingfield Rise DE3 . . **24** B3
Links Cl DE24 . . . . . **45** C4
Linnet Cl DE21 . . . . **22** B2
Linnet Hill DE21 . . . **33** B3
Liskeard Dr DE22 . . **11** C4
Lismore Ct **6** DE24 . **45** A3
Lister Cl DE3 . . . . . . **26** A3
Liston Dr DE22 . . . . **18** B4
LITCHURCH **28** B3
Litchurch La DE24 . . **28** B2
Litchurch St DE1 . . . **61** C1
LITTLE CHESTER . . **18** C3
Littledale Cl DE21 . . **15** B3
Little Derby Hill
DE65 . . . . **42** B2
LITTLE EATON **10** A4
Little Eaton Prim Sch
DE21 . . . . **10** A3
Little Longstone Cl
DE3 . . . . **25** B2
Little Meadow Rd
DE73 . . . . **48** A2
Little Moorside
DE72 . . . . **51** B3
LITTLEOVER **35** A4
Littleover Com Sch
DE23 . . . . **34** B4
Littleover Cres
DE23 . . . . **26** C1
Littleover La DE23 . . **36** A4
Little Woodbury Dr
DE23 . . . . **34** B2
Litton Cl DE56 . . . . . **3** A3
Litton Dr DE21 . . . . **31** B3
Liverpool St **4**
DE21 . . . . **20** A4
Liversage Almshouses
DE1 . . . . **61** C2
Liversage Pl DE1 . . . **61** C1
Liversage St DE1 . . . **61** C2
Livingstone Rd
DE23 . . . . **27** A1
Lloyd St DE22 . . . . . . **17** C1
Loake Cl **1** DE73 . . **59** A3
Lochinvar Cl DE21 . . **31** B4
Lockington Cl DE73 **47** C2
Locko Ct DE21 . . . . . **21** C1
Locko Rd DE21 . . . . **22** A3
Lock Up Yd DE1 . . . . **60** B3
Lockwood Rd DE24 . . **11** C4
Locomotive Way
DE24 . . . . **28** C3

Lodge Cl
Duffield DE56 . . . . **7** B2
Etwall DE65 . . . . **58** C3
Lodge Dr DE56 . . . . . . **2** A3
Lodge Est DE72 . . . . **51** B2
Lodge La
Derby DE1 . . . . **60** A4
Derby, Spondon
DE21 . . . . **30** C4
Lodge Mews DE72 . . **51** B2
Lodge St DE72 . . . . . . **40** C1
Lodge Way DE3 . . . . **24** C1
Loganberry Ct
DE24 . . . . **38** A4
Lombard St DE22 . . . **16** B2
Lomond Ave DE24 . . **45** C2
London Rd DE23,
DE24 . . . . **28** C2
Long Bridge La
DE24 . . . . **37** C4
Long Croft DE72 . . . **51** A3
Longdons Row
DE21 . . . . **21** C1
Longford Cl DE22 . . **11** C1
Longford St DE23 . . **18** A4
Longlands La DE65 . **42** C1
Longlands Mews
DE65 . . . . **42** C1
Longley La DE21 . . . **21** C2
Long Row DE56 . . . . **2** B2
Long Row Prim Sch
DE56 . . . . **2** B2
Longshaw Gdns
DE24 . . . . **38** C2
Longs Mill **4** DE1 . . **60** A4
Longstock Cl DE21 . **14** A1
Longstone Rise
DE56 . . . . **3** A4
Longstone Wlk DE1 **61** A2
Longthorpe Cl
DE23 . . . . **34** C3
Lonsdale Pl DE22 . . **26** C4
Loom Cl DE56 . . . . . . **3** B3
Lord St DE24 . . . . . . **37** C2
Lorne St DE22 . . . . . **27** B3
Lorraine Cl DE24 . . **47** B3
Loscoe Rd DE21 . . . . **14** C1
Lothian Pl
Castle Donington
DE74 . . . . **53** A1
Derby DE21 . . . . **19** C3
Lothlorien Cl DE23 . . **35** A3
Loudon St DE23 . . . . **27** C3
Loudoun Pl DE74 . . . **53** A2
Lousie Greaves La
DE21 . . . . **22** A2
Louvain Rd DE22,
DE23 . . . . **26** C2
Lower Dale Rd
DE23 . . . . **27** B2
Lower Eley St DE1 . . **61** A1
Lower Gn DE65 . . . . **43** A1
Lower Hall Cl DE56 . . **5** A1
Lower St DE22 . . . . . **16** B4
Lowe St DE24. . . . . . **38** A2
Lowlands Rd DE56 . . **3** B4
Lows Ct DE73 . . . . . . **48** B2
Loxley Cl DE21 . . . . **15** A2
Loxton Ct DE3 . . . . . **24** C3
Loyne Cl DE24 . . . . . **45** C2
Luccombe Dr DE24 . **39** C1
Lucerne Rd DE21 . . . **15** B3
Ludgate Wlk DE22 . . **16** A2
Ludlow Cl DE21 . . . . **22** B1
Lulworth Cl DE23 . . **35** C2
Lundie Cl DE24 . . . . **45** A2
Lupin Cl DE21 . . . . . **15** B3

Lychgate Cl DE21 . . **13** C2
Lydstep Cl DE21 . . . **15** B2
Lyndhurst Gr DE21 . . **20** C1
Lyndhurst St DE23 . . **27** C2
Lynton St DE22 . . . . **27** A4
Lynwood Rd DE24 . . **45** C4
Lysander Dr DE73 . . **47** B1
Lytham Cl DE21 . . . . **13** C1
Lyttelton St DE22 . . **17** B1

M

MacAulay St DE24 . . **36** C1
McAuley Ct DE1 . . . . **60** B4
McGough Mews
DE24 . . . . **36** C1
Mackenzie St DE22 . **17** B1
Macklin St DE1 . . . . **61** B3
MACKWORTH **16** A4
Mackworth Rd DE1,
DE22 . . . . **18** A2
McNeil Gr DE72 . . . . **40** C1
Macready Pl DE24 . . **38** B3
Madeley St DE3 . . . . **24** C1
Madeley St DE23 . . . **27** C2
Madison Ave DE21 . . **20** C4
Magdala Cotts DE56 . **7** B4
Magee Cl DE1 . . . . . . **61** C1
Maidstone Dr DE24 . **38** B1
Maidwell Cl DE56 . . . **3** B4
Main Ave DE22 . . . . . . **9** A1
Maine Dr DE21 . . . . . **20** C2
Main St
Breaston DE72 . . . . . . **41** C2
Etwall DE65 . . . . **58** B3
Findern DE65 . . . . **43** A1
King's Newton DE73. . **59** C4
Maize Cl DE23 . . . . . . **34** C2
Makeney Rd
Duffield DE56 . . . . **7** C1
Holbrook DE56 . . . . . . **5** A1
Malcolm Gr DE23 . . . **34** A4
Malcolm St DE23 . . . **28** A2
Malham Rd DE23 . . . **34** B2
Malin Cl DE24 . . . . . . **39** A1
Mallard Wlk DE3 . . . **33** B4
Maltby Cl **2** DE22 . . **12** B2
Maltings The
Derby DE1 . . . . **61** B2
Derby DE22 . . . . **17** C2
Malton Pl DE21 . . . . **13** C1
Malvern Cl DE3 . . . . **24** C3
Malvern Way **3**
DE21 . . . . **13** C1
Manchester St
DE22 . . . . **17** C2
Mandarin Way
DE24 . . . . **38** B4
Manifold Dr DE24. . . **39** A4
Manor Ave DE23 . . . **26** B3
Manor Farm Barns
DE21 . . . . **14** A3
Manor Farm Mews
DE72 . . . . **51** B3
Manor Farm Rd
DE72 . . . . **51** B3
Manor Park Ct DE3 . **26** A3
Manor Park Way
DE3 . . . . **26** A3
Manor Pk DE72 . . . . **32** A1
Manor Rd
Belper DE56 . . . . **2** B1
Borrowash DE72 . . . . . **31** C1
Chellaston DE73. . . . . **47** C1
Derby DE23 . . . . **26** B2
Mansfield Rd DE1,
DE21 . . . . **60** B4

Mansfields Croft
DE65 . . . . **58** B3
Mansfield St DE1 . . . **60** B5
Maple Ave DE23 . . . . **35** C2
Maplebeck Ct DE1 . . **60** B5
Maple Dr
Aston-on-T DE72 . . . . **51** A2
Belper DE56 . . . . **4** C4
Chellaston DE73 . . . . **48** A2
Derby, Boulton
DE24 . . . . **38** C2
Maple Gr DE22 . . . . . . **8** B1
Maple Rd DE74 . . . . **53** A3
Mapleton Ave DE21 . **14** B1
Mapleton Rd DE72 . . **40** C2
Marchington Cl
DE22 . . . . **12** A1
Marcus St DE1 . . . . . **18** C3
Maree Cl DE24 . . . . . **45** B4
Marfleet Cl DE3 . . . . **24** C3
Margaret Ave DE21 . **20** B1
Margaret St DE1 . . . . **60** B5
Margreave Rd DE21 . **20** B3
Marigold Cl DE21 . . **15** A3
Marina Dr
Derby, Allenton
DE24 . . . . **38** A1
Derby, Spondon
DE21 . . . . **21** C1
Marjorie Rd DE21 . . **20** B4
MARKEATON **17** A4
Markeaton La DE22 . **17** A4
Markeaton Pk★
DE22 . . . . **17** C3
Markeaton Prim Sch
DE22 . . . . **17** C3
Markeaton St DE22 . **18** A2
Market Head DE56 . . **2** C1
Market Pl
Belper DE56 . . . . **2** C1
Derby DE1 . . . . **60** B3
Melbourne DE73. . . . . **59** B2
Market St
Castle Donington
DE74 . . . . **53** B2
Draycott DE72 . . . . . . **40** C1
Markham Cl DE21 . . **14** B2
Mark's Cl DE23 . . . . **35** C2
Marlborough Dr
DE56 . . . . **3** B3
Marlborough Rd
Breaston DE72 . . . . . . **41** C2
Derby DE24. . . . . **37** B3
Marlowe Ct DE23 . . **36** B2
Marquis Gdns DE21 . **50** A4
Marsden Cl DE56 . . . **7** B2
Marsden St DE24 . . . **38** A3
Marshaw Cl DE3 . . . **25** A1
Marshgreen Cl
DE24 . . . . **39** C1
Marsh La DE56 . . . . . **3** A3
Marsh Lane Cres
DE56 . . . . **3** A2
Marston Cl
Belper DE56 . . . . **3** B4
Derby DE23. . . . . **35** C1
Martindale Ct DE56 . . **3** B2
Martin Dr DE21 . . . . **20** C4
Maryland Rd DE21 . . **21** A2
Marylebone Cres
DE22 . . . . **16** C2
Masefield Ave
DE23 . . . . **36** A3
Masons Place Bsns Pk
DE21 . . . . **19** C2

Masson Wlk DE22.....**27** A4
Matlock Ho DE21 ... **31** A3
Matlock Rd DE21 ... **14** B1
Matthew St DE24 .... **38** B2
Matthew Way DE23 . **34** A3
Max Rd DE21 .... **20** B4
Maxwell Ave DE7 ... **17** C4
Mayfair Cres DE22 .. **16** B2
Mayfair Ct DE56 .... **7** B3
Mayfield Ave DE56 ... **6** B2
Mayfield Rd DE21... **20** A3
Maylands
DE72.............. **32** A1
Maypole La DE23 ... **34** A3
May St DE22......... **27** B3
Maytree Cl DE21.... **15** B3
Mayvale Gr DE22 ... **26** B4
Mead Cl DE24 ...... **45** C4
Meadow Brook Cl
DE23.............. **34** B2
Meadow Cl
Derby DE21........ **31** A4
Draycott DE72..... **40** C1
Findern DE65 ...... **43** A2
Meadow Cres DE74 . **56** B4
Meadow Ct
Belper DE56 .... **2** B2
5 Derby DE3 ..... **24** C1
Kilburn DE56....... **6** B1
Meadow Farm Com
Prim Sch DE21 ... **29** C4
Meadowgrass Cl
DE23.............. **35** A2
Meadow La
Derby, Chaddesden
DE21.............. **20** B1
Derby DE1, DE21.....**60** D3
Meadowlark Gr
DE21.............. **14** C1
Meadow Nook
DE24.............. **39** B4
Meadow Rd
Derby DE1.........**60** C3
Derby, Wilmorton DE21,
DE24.............. **29** B1
Meadows Croft DE56. **7** A2
Meadows Ind Est The
DE21.............. **19** C1
Meadows Prim Sch
DE56.............. **7** A2
Meadow Vale DE56... **7** A2
Meadow View DE56 .. **2** B1
Meadow View Cl
DE21.............. **15** A3
Meadow Way DE73 .. **48** A1
Mear Dr DE72 .... **32** A1
Meath Ave DE21 .... **30** A4
Medina Cl DE24..... **39** C1
Medway Dr DE22 .... **9** C1
Meerbrook Cl DE21 . **14** C1
Megaloughton La
DE21.............. **30** B3
Melandra Ct DE22 .. **27** A4
Melbourn Cl DE56 ... **7** B2
MELBOURNE **59** B3
Melbourne Cl
Belper DE56 .... **4** B4
Derby DE22.........**11** C2
Derby, Mickleover
DE3.............. **25** B3
Melbourne Ct DE24 **29** A4
Melbourne Hall &
Gdns★ DE73.....**59** C2
Melbourne Ho
DE21.............. **31** A3

Melbourne Inf Sch
DE73.............**59** A2
Melbourne Jun Sch
DE73.............**59** A2
Melbourne St DE1 .. **61** B1
Melbreak Cl DE3.... **25** A1
Melfort Cl DE24.....**45** C2
Mellor's La DE56.... **5** A1
Mellor St DE24 ..... **38** A2
Melrose Cl DE24.... **45** B2
Melton Ave
Derby DE23.........**35** B2
Melbourne DE73.....**59** A3
Melton Ct DE22..... **18** A2
Melville St DE65 .... **58** B2
Memorial Rd DE22.. **11** B3
Mendip Ct DE21 .... **14** A2
Menin Rd DE22 ..... **11** B2
Mercaston Rd DE21. **20** B4
Merchant Ave DE21 **30** C4
Merchants Cnr
DE22.............. **18** A2
Merchant St DE22 .. **18** A2
Mercian Mews
DE21..............**30** C4
Merion Ct DE23 .... **25** C1
Merlin Cl DE56 ..... **3** B3
Merlin Gn DE24..... **45** A4
Merlin Way DE21 ... **33** A3
Merridale Rd DE23.. **35** B4
Merrill Coll DE24 ... **47** C4
Merrill Coll (Lower
Site) DE24.........**38** A2
Merrill Way DE24 ... **37** C1
Merrybower Cl
DE24.............. **45** A3
Merthyr Ct DE21.... **15** A2
Metcalfe Cl DE24 ... **39** A4
Meteor Ctr The
DE21.............. **13** B1
Mews Ct DE3 .... **24** C4
Mews The DE75..... **59** A2
Meynell Ct DE22 ... **11** B2
Meynell St DE23 .... **27** B1
Michelle Cl DE24 ... **44** C3
Michigan Cl DE21... **21** B1
Micklecroft Gdns
DE23.............. **34** A3
MICKLEOVER..... **25** A2
Mickleover Ho DE3 . **33** C4
Mickleover Manor
DE3.............. **24** B1
Mickleover Prim Sch
DE3.............. **24** C2
Mickleross Cl DE3 .. **24** C4
Middlebeck Cl
DE73.............**47** C2
Middle Mill **2** DE1. **60** A4
Middleton Ave
DE23.............. **26** B2
Middleton Dr DE23 . **26** B2
Middleton St DE23.. **27** C1
Midland Pl DE1.....**61** D2
Midland Rd DE1 ....**61** D1
Midland View **7**
DE56.............. **2** B1
Midway DE22.......**12** A2
Milbank Cl DE21 .... **14** B2
Milburn Gdns DE21 . **15** A3
Milbury Cl DE21 .... **14** B2
Mile Ash La DE22... **12** B1
MILFORD...........**4** B1
Milford Com Prim Sch
DE56.............. **4** A1
Milford Rd DE56 .... **7** B3
Milford St **4** DE1 .. **18** B3
Milford The DE1.... **18** B1
Millbank Dr DE56... **4** C4

Mill Cl
Borrowash DE72.....**32** B1
Findern DE65 ......**43** A2
Kilburn DE56........ **6** B1
Mill Cliff DE3 ...... **24** C4
Milldale Ct DE56.... **3** A1
Milldale Rd DE21 ... **31** B3
Millennium Way
DE24.............. **29** A4
Millers Ct DE1 ..... **60** B4
Millers Dale Cl DE56 . **3** B3
Mill Gate DE22......**18** A2
Mill Hill DE1 ...... **48** C4
Mill Hill La DE1,
DE23.............. **61** B1
Mill Hill Rd DE23... **61** A1
Millhouse DE72 .... **41** A1
Mill La
Belper DE56 .... **3** A1
Derby DE3.........**24** C4
Mill Meadow Way
DE65.............. **58** B3
Mill Moor Cl DE73 .. **47** C2
Millom Pl DE21 .... **13** C1
Mill Row DE21...... **21** C1
Mills Cl DE72 ...... **40** C1
Mill St
Belper DE56 .... **2** C2
Derby DE1..........**18** A2
Mill View DE56...... **2** B3
Milner Ave DE72.... **40** C1
Milton Cl DE3 ..... **24** B3
Milton St DE22 .... **26** C4
Mimosa Cres DE23.. **36** A1
Minster Rd DE21.... **14** A2
Minton Rd DE74 .... **52** C2
Misterton Ct DE22 .. **12** A2
Mitcham Wlk DE22 . **16** C2
Mitchells Cl DE65 ... **58** A3
Moat The DE74 ..... **53** B2
Moira Cl DE21...... **20** C3
Moira Dale DE74.... **53** C1
Moira St DE73 ..... **59** A2
Molineux St DE23 .. **28** A2
Monarch Dr DE21... **15** C3
Moncrieff Cres
DE21.............. **20** C4
Mondello Dr DE24 . **39** B2
Monks Cl DE24 ..... **44** C3
Monk St DE22 ..... **61** A2
Monmouth St DE21. **19** C2
Monsal Dr DE21.... **31** B3
Montague Way
DE73.............. **47** B2
Monteith Pl DE74... **53** B2
Montfort Mews
DE74.............. **53** B2
Montpelier DE22 ... **8** B3
Montrose Cl DE24 .. **45** B4
Monyash Cl DE21.... **20** C4
Monyash Way DE56.. **3** A3
Moor Dr DE24 ...... **39** A1
Moor End DE21 .... **22** B2
Moore St DE23 ..... **27** C3
Moorfield Rd DE56... **5** A1
Moorgate DE22......**16** A2
Moorhead Ave
DE24.............. **38** B1
Moorhead Prim Sch
DE24.............. **38** B2
Moor La
Aston-on-T DE72....**51** B3
Derby DE24........**37** B2
Ockbrook DE72.....**23** B2
Moorland Rd DE3... **24** C3
Moorpool Cres DE56. **5** A1
Moor Rise DE56 .... **3** A1

Moorside Cres
DE24.............. **45** C4
Moorside Gdns
DE72.............. **51** C4
Moorside La DE56 ... **5** A1
Moor St DE21........ **22** A1
Moorway DE21 .... **14** A4
Moorway Croft
DE23.............. **35** A3
Moorway La DE23... **35** A2
Moorways Sports Ctr
DE24.............. **37** C2
Moray Wlk DE21.... **19** B4
Morden Gn DE22....**16** C2
Morefern Dr DE21 .. **14** B2
Morledge DE1.......**60** C3
Morleston St DE23.. **61** C1
Morley Cl DE56 ..... **3** D4
Morley Gdns DE21 .. **21** A4
Morley Hall Prep Sch
DE7.............. **15** A1
Morley Ho
Derby, Alvaston
DE24.............. **38** C3
1 Derby, Mickleover
DE3 ....**24** C1
Morley La DE7,
DE21.............. **10** C4
Morley Mews DE21 . **20** C3
Morley Rd DE21 .... **21** A4
Morley St DE22..... **27** C1
Morlich Dr DE24.... **36** A1
Morningside Cl
DE24.............. **47** A4
Mornington Cres
DE22.............. **17** A2
Morpeth Gdns
DE21.............. **13** C2
Morrell Wood Dr
DE56.............. **3** C3
Mortimer St DE24 .. **37** B3
Mosedale Cl DE24 .. **38** B4
Moss St DE22.......**27** A3
Mossvale Dr DE23 .. **34** C2
Mostyn Ave DE23 .. **26** C1
Mottistone Cl DE24 . **39** C1
Moulbourn Dr DE56.. **7** A3
Moult Ave DE21.....**31** A4
Moulton Cl DE24 ... **3** C3
Mountbatten Cl
DE24.............. **47** B4
Mount Carmel St
DE23.............. **61** C1
Mountfield Way
DE24.............. **49** A4
Mountford Cl DE21 . **15** A2
MOUNT PLEASANT . **2** A4
Mount Pleasant
DE74.............. **53** B1
Mount Pleasant Dr
DE56.............. **2** A3
Mount St DE1 ..... **61** B1
Mowbray Gdns
DE24.............. **37** B3
Mowbray St DE24... **37** C4
Moy Ave DE24 ..... **45** C2
Moyne Gdns DE73 .. **50** C4
Muirfield Dr DE3 ... **25** B2
Mulberries Ct DE22 **12** A4
Mulberry Cl DE56.... **3** A1
Mulberry Way DE72 **51** A1
Mull Ct **3** DE24.... **45** A3
Mullion Pl DE24 ... **39** A1
Mundy Cl DE1......**18** A2
Mundy St DE1 ..... **18** A2
Munro Ct DE24 .... **45** B4
Murray Park Com Sch
DE3.............. **25** B4

Murray Rd DE3 ..... **25** B4
Murray St DE24 .... **37** C4
Muswell Rd DE22 ... **16** A1
Myers Cl DE24......**45** C4

N

Nailers Way DE56.... **3** B3
Nairn Ave DE21.....**19** C3
Nairn Cl DE24......**45** A3
Namur Cl DE22 .... **26** B3
Napier Cl DE3 ..... **25** A4
Napier St DE22 .... **17** B1
Napoleon Pk DE24..**38** A3
Naseby Cl DE3 ..... **24** B3
Naseby Rd DE56 .... **3** C2
Navigation Home Park
DE24.............. **38** A4
Navigation Home Pk
DE24.............. **29** A1
Nearwood Dr DE21 . **14** A3
Neilson St DE24 .... **38** B3
Nelson Cl DE3 ..... **25** B3
Nelson St DE1...... **61** D1
Nerissa Cl DE73.... **47** B2
Nesfield Cl DE24 ... **39** B3
Ness Wlk DE22 .... **12** A3
Nestor Cl DE73 .... **47** A2
Nether Cl DE56 .... **7** B4
Netherclose St
DE23.............. **27** C1
Nether Park Dr
DE22.............. **11** B1
Netherside Dr DE73. **48** B2
Netherwood Ct
DE22.............. **11** B3
Nettlefold Cres
DE73.............. **59** B4
Nettleton Cl DE23... **34** C2
Nevinson Ave DE23 **35** C3
Nevinson Dr DE23 .. **35** C3
Nevis Cl DE24......**45** A2
Newark Rd DE21.... **13** C2
Newbold Ave DE72.. **32** B1
Newbold Cl DE73... **47** C2
Newbold Dr DE74... **53** B3
Newborough Rd
DE24.............. **39** B2
New Breck Rd DE56.. **2** C1
Newbridge Cres
DE24.............. **47** B4
Newbury St DE24 .. **38** A4
Newchase Bsns Pk
DE23.............. **28** B3
New City Park Homes
DE24.............. **29** C1
New City Pk Homes
DE24.............. **38** C4
Newdigate St DE23 . **36** C4
Newgate Cl DE73 ... **48** B2
Newhaven Rd DE21 . **21** A2
New Inn La DE21.... **10** A3
Newland St DE1..... **60** A3
Newlyn Dr DE23 ... **36** B4
Newmarket Ct
DE24.............. **29** A1
Newmarket Dr
DE24.............. **38** A4
New Mount Cl
DE23.............. **35** C1
New Park Pl DE24 .. **28** C3
Newport Cl DE24 ... **39** B1
Newquay Pl DE24... **39** B1
New Rd
Belper DE56 .... **2** B1
Derby DE22........**12** C1
New St
Derby DE1..........**61** C2

New St continued
Draycott La DE72 . . . . . . **40** C1
Little Eaton DE21 . . . . **10** A4
Ockbrook DE72 . . . . **32** B4
Newstead Ave DE21. **20** B2
Newton Cl DE56 . . . . . **3** B4
Newton's Wlk DE22 **18** A4
Newton Wonder Ct
DE73 . . . . **59** B4
NEW YORK **59** A2
NEW ZEALAND **17** B1
New Zealand La
DE56 . . . . **7** B1
New Zealand Sq
DE22 . . . . **17** B1
Nicholas Cl DE21 . . . **22** A2
Nicola Gdns DE23. . . **45** A4
Nidderdale Ct DE24 **39** C2
Nightingale Bsns Pk
DE24 . . . . **37** C4
Nightingale Jun & Inf
Schs DE24. . . . . **37** B3
Nightingale Mews
DE1 . . . . **61** D2
Nightingale Rd
DE24 . . . . **37** B4
Noble St DE1 . . . . **61** D1
Noel-Baker Com Sch
DE24 . . . . **47** C4
Noel St DE1 . . . . **17** C2
Nook The DE56 . . . . . **5** A1
Nooning La DE72 . . . **40** A2
Norbury Cl DE22 . . . **11** C1
Norbury Cres DE23 **35** B1
Norbury Ct **2** DE22 **11** C2
Norbury Way DE56. . . **3** B4
Norfolk Gdns DE22. . **18** B4
Norfolk St DE23 . . . . **28** A2
Norman Ave DE23 . . **36** A3
NORMANTON **36** B3
Normanton House
Prim Sch DE23 . . **36** B4
Normanton Jun Sch
DE23 . . . . **36** A3
Normanton La
DE23 . . . . **35** B4
Normanton Lodge
DE23 . . . . **36** A4
Normanton Rd DE1 . **61** B1
Normanton Village Inf
Sch DE23 . . . . **36** B4
Northacre Rd DE21 . **15** A2
North Ave
Derby, Darley Abbey
DE22 . . . . **12** C3
Derby DE3. . . . . **25** A2
North Cl DE3 . . . . . . **25** A3
Northfield
Derby DE24. . . . . **45** A3
Kilburn DE56. . . . . **6** A4
Northgate DE1 . . . . . **60** B4
Northmead Dr DE3 . **26** A3
North Mill DE56 . . . . . **2** B3
North Par DE1 . . . . . **60** B4
North Row DE22 . . . **12** C1
North St
Derby DE1. . . . . **60** B5
Derby DE23. . . . . **26** B2
Melbourne DE73. . . . . **59** A2
Northumberland St
DE23 . . . . **27** B2
North View DE23 . . . **26** B1
Northway Dr DE1 . . **27** A4
Northwood Ave
DE21 . . . . **20** A3
Norwich St DE21. . . . **19** C3
Norwood Cl DE22 . . **16** C1
Nothills DE73 . . . . . . **48** A1

Nottingham East
Midlands Airport
Aeropark ★ DE74. . . **56** A3
Nottingham Rd
Belper DE56 . . . . **3** A2
Borrowash DE72. . . . **32** C2
Derby, Chaddesden
DE21 . . . . **20** A2
Derby DE1, DE21 . . . **60** C4
Derby, Spondon
DE21 . . . . **31** A3
Nunsfield Dr DE24 . . **39** A3
Nun's St DE1 . . . . **18** A2
Nursery Cl DE72 . . . . **32** A2
Nutwood Cl DE22 . . **12** C3

O

Oadby Rise DE23 . . . **36** A2
Oak Cl
Derby DE22. . . . . **12** A4
Duffield DE56 . . . . **7** B1
Ockbrook DE72. . . . . **23** B1
Oak Cres DE23 . . . . . **35** B4
Oakdale Gdns DE21 **15** A3
Oak Dr
Derby, Boulton
DE24 . . . . **38** C2
Derby DE3. . . . . **25** A2
Oakfields Gr DE21 . . **30** C3
Oakham Cl DE21. . . . **13** C1
Oakhurst Cl DE56. . . . **2** A4
Oaklands Ave DE23 . **35** B1
Oaklands Rd DE65 . . **58** C3
Oaklands Way DE73. **59** B3
Oakleigh Ave DE21. . **20** B2
Oakover Dr DE22 . . . **11** C2
Oak Rd DE72 . . . . **49** C4
Oakridge DE21 . . . . . **21** A3
Oakridge Pk DE74 . . **53** A3
Oakside Way DE21. . **15** A3
Oak St DE23 . . . . **27** C2
Oaktree Ave DE24 . . **37** A3
Oak Tree Ct DE72 . . **32** C1
Oakvale Ho DE23 . . . **27** C2
OAKWOOD **14** C2
Oakwood Cl DE65. . . **45** A2
Oakwood District Ctr
DE21 . . . . **14** C1
Oakwood Dr DE21 . . **15** A2
Oakwood Inf Sch
DE24 . . . . **38** C2
Oakwood Jun Sch
DE24 . . . . **38** C2
Oberon Cl DE73. . . . . **47** B1
OCKBROOK. **23** C1
Octavia Cl DE73. . . . . **47** B2
Offerton Ave DE23 . . **36** B4
Old Barn Cl DE21 . . . **10** B4
Oldbury Cl DE21 . . . . **14** C2
Old Chester Rd
DE1 . . . . **18** C4
Old Church Ct DE22 . . **8** A1
Old Hall Ave
Derby, Alvaston
DE24 . . . . **39** A3
Derby DE23. . . . . **26** A1
Duffield DE56 . . . . **7** B2
Old Hall Mills Bsns Pk
DE21 . . . . **10** A3
Old Hall Rd DE23 . . . **26** B1
Old La DE22 . . . . **12** C2
Old Mansfield Rd
DE21 . . . . **13** B1
Old Mill Cl DE56 . . . . . **7** B2

Old School Mews
DE72 . . . . **51** B3
Old Station Cl DE65 . **58** B3
Old Vicarage Cl
DE21 . . . . **26** B1
Old Vicarage La
DE22 . . . . **8** A1
Old Vicarage Sch The
DE22 . . . . **12** C3
Olive Gr DE21. . . . . . . **20** B1
Olive St DE22 . . . . **27** A4
Olivier St DE23 . . . . . **28** A1
Olton Rd DE3 . . . . **24** B4
Onslow Rd DE3. . . . . **25** A4
Opal Cl DE21 . . . . **14** C2
OPENWOODGATE . . . **3** C1
Openwoodgate
DE56 . . . . **3** C1
Openwood Rd DE56. . **3** C1
Orchard Ave DE74 . . **53** A1
Orchard Cl
Belper DE56 . . . . **4** C2
Breadsall DE21. . . . . . **13** C4
Derby DE23. . . . . **35** B3
Elvaston DE24. . . . . . . **49** A4
Melbourne DE73. . . . . **59** A2
Ockbrook DE72. . . . . **59** A2
Orchard Com Prim
Sch DE74. . . . . **53** A1
Orchard Cotts DE56. . **3** A2
Orchard Ct DE21. . . . **22** A1
Orchard St
Derby DE1. . . . . **60** A4
Derby, Mickleover
DE3 . . . . **24** C1
Orchards The DE22. . **11** C3
Orchard The **6**
DE56 . . . . **2** B2
Orchard Way DE73 . . **47** C2
Ordish Ave DE21 . . . **20** B1
Oregon Way DE21 . . **21** B2
Oriel Cl DE1 . . . . **61** C1
Orient Way DE24. . . . **29** A2
Orkney Cl DE24 . . . . . **45** A3
Orly Ave DE74 . . . . . . **56** A4
Ormskirk Rise DE21. **31** B4
Orton Way DE56 . . . . **3** A4
Osborne Ct DE21 . . . **13** C4
Osborne Rd DE23 . . . **28** B3
Osborne St DE23 . . . **61** D1
Osiers Cl DE22. . . . . . **11** B1
OSMASTON. **37** B4
Osmaston Park Ind Est
DE24 . . . . **38** A4
Osmaston Park Rd
DE23, DE24. . . . . **37** B3
Osmaston Rd DE23,
DE24 . . . . **28** A2
Osmaton Park Ind Est
DE24 . . . . **28** C1
Osprey Cl DE24 . . . . . **45** B2
Osterly Gn DE22 . . . . **16** C1
Oswestry Cl DE21. . . **15** A3
Othello Dr DE73 . . . . **47** A2
Otterburn Dr DE22. . **11** B2
Otter St DE1. . . . . **18** C3
Oulton Cl DE24 . . . . . **47** A4
Outram Cl DE72 . . . . **32** A1
Outram Way DE24 . . **45** B2
Oval Cl DE23 . . . . **35** B4
Overdale Rd DE23 . . **27** A2
Over La DE56 . . . . **3** D3
Overstone Cl DE56. . . **3** C2
Owlers La DE23. . . . . **26** B2
Owlswick Cl DE23. . . **34** C4
Oxenhope Cl DE23 . . **34** A3
Oxford St
Derby DE1. . . . . **61** C1

Oxford St continued
Derby, Spondon
DE21 . . . . **22** A1
Oxwich Ct DE21. . . . . **15** A2

P

Pack Horse Rd
DE73 . . . . **59** B3
Paddock Cl DE74 . . . **52** C1
Paddock Croft **9**
DE21 . . . . **14** B2
Paddock The
Elvaston DE24. . . . . . . **49** A4
Holbrook DE56. . . . . . . **5** A1
Ockbrook DE72. . . . . **32** B4
Padley Cl DE22 . . . . . . **9** B1
Padstow Cl **13**
DE24 . . . . **45** A3
Padstow Rd DE24 . . . **39** B1
Palatine Gr DE23 . . . **34** B3
Palladium Dr DE23. . **34** C2
Pall Mall DE21. . . . . . **14** A4
Palm Cl DE21 . . . . **25** C1
Palmerston Ct
DE73 . . . . **59** B2
Palmerston St
DE23 . . . . **27** A1
Parade The **4** DE3. . **24** C1
Parcel Terr DE22 . . . . **17** C1
Pares Way DE72 . . . . **23** B1
Park Ave DE74 . . . . . . **52** C1
Park Cl
Kilburn DE56. . . . . **6** B2
Little Eaton DE21 . . . . . **9** C4
Park Dr DE23 . . . . **26** B1
Parker Cl DE1 . . . . . . **60** A4
Parker Ctr DE21 . . . . **19** A4
Parker St DE1 . . . . . . **18** B3
Park Farm Ctr
DE22 . . . . **11** C2
Park Farm Dr DE22 . **11** C2
Parkfields Dr DE22. . **18** A4
Parkgate DE23 . . . . . **28** A2
Park Gr DE22 . . . . **18** A3
Park Hill Dr DE23 . . . **36** B3
Park Ho DE56. . . . . **2** C1
Park La
Castle Donington
DE74 . . . . **52** B1
Derby, Allestree
DE22 . . . . **12** B4
Derby, Normanton Park
DE23 . . . . **27** C1
Parklands Dr DE73. . **50** C4
Park Leys Ct DE21 . . **31** A4
Park Mews DE22 . . . **18** B4
Park Rd
Belper DE56 . . . . **4** B4
Derby DE3. . . . . **24** C2
Derby, Spondon
DE21 . . . . **21** C1
Duffield DE56 . . . . **7** A2
Park Side DE56 . . . . . . **2** C1
Parkside Rd DE21. . . **21** A2
Park St DE1 . . . . **61** D2
Parkstone Ct DE3. . . **24** B2
Park The DE56 . . . . . . **7** B2
Parkview DE21 . . . . . **10** A4
Park View DE72. . . . . **51** B2
Park View Cl DE22 . . **12** B4
Park View Ho DE21. . **19** B2
Parkview Prim Sch
DE21 . . . . **14** C2
Parkway DE73 . . . . . . **47** B1
Park Way DE65 . . . . . **58** C3
Parliament Cl DE22 . **27** A4
Parliament St DE22 . **27** A4

New−Phi 73

Partridge Way DE3 . **25** C3
Pastures Ave DE23 . . **34** B3
Pastures Hill DE23 . . **26** A1
Pastures The DE56. . . **7** B3
Paterson Ave DE21. . **21** A2
Patmore Sq DE23 . . . **36** B3
Patten Ct DE24 . . . . . **36** C1
Patterdale Rd DE24 **29** C1
Pavilion Rd DE23 . . . **35** B4
Paxton Cl DE3 . . . . . . **24** B1
Payne St DE22. . . . . . **17** C2
Peach St DE22. . . . . . **17** C1
Peacock Gr DE23 . . . **35** A2
Peak Dr DE23, DE24 . **36** C3
Pearl Cl DE21. . . . . . . **14** C2
PEARTREE **37** A4
Peartree Cl DE74 . . . **53** A1
Pear Tree Com Jun
Sch DE23. . . . . **27** C1
Pear Tree Cres
DE23 . . . . **36** C4
Peartree Ct
Derby DE21. . . . . **13** C1
Etwall DE65 . . . . **58** B3
Pear Tree Rd DE23 . . **27** C1
Peartree Sta DE23 . . **37** A3
Peckham Gdns
DE22 . . . . **16** C1
Peebles Cl DE24 . . . . **45** B3
Peel St DE22 . . . . **17** C2
Peers Cl DE21 . . . . . . **15** A2
Peet St DE22 . . . . **27** A4
Peggs Wlk DE23 . . . . **36** A3
Pegwell Cl DE23 . . . . **35** C3
Pelham St DE22 . . . . **27** B4
Pembroke St DE21. . **19** C4
Penalton Cl DE24 . . . **38** A2
Pencroft Gr DE23 . . . **35** B1
Pendennis Cl DE24 . **39** A2
Pendlebury Dr DE3 . **25** A1
Pendleside Way
DE23 . . . . **34** A3
Penge Rd DE22 . . . . . **16** C3
Penhaligan's Cl
DE73 . . . . **47** C1
Peniston Rise DE73 **59** A2
Penn La DE73 . . . . . . **59** B2
Penn St DE56. . . . . **2** C2
Pennycress Cl
DE23 . . . . **34** C3
Penny Long La
DE22 . . . . **18** A4
Penrhyn Ave DE23 . . **26** C1
Penrith Pl DE21 . . . . **13** C2
Pentagon The DE21. **19** B2
Pentewen Cl DE22. . **12** A2
Pentland Cl DE21 . . **14** C2
Penzance Rd DE24. . **39** A1
Percy St DE22 . . . . . . **27** A3
Peregrine Cl DE24 . . **45** A4
Perth Cl DE3 . . . . **25** A4
Perth St DE21 . . . . . . **13** C1
Peter Baines Ind Est
DE22 . . . . **61** A1
Peterborough St
DE21 . . . . **20** A4
Peterhouse Terr **1**
DE23 . . . . **27** C2
Peterlee Pl DE24 . . . **38** C1
Petersham Dr DE24 **39** B2
Peveril Ave DE72 . . . **32** B2
Peveril St DE24 . . . . . **37** C2
Pheasant Field Dr
DE21 . . . . **22** C2
Philips Croft DE56 . . . **7** B3

Phoenix St DE1...... **60** B4
Pickburns Gdns
DE56............... **6** A2
Pickering Rise
DE21............... **13** C1
Pickford's House
Mus★ DE1....... **18** B1
Pilgrims Way DE24.. **44** C3
Pilsley Cl DE56.... **3** B4
Pimlico DE22....... **17** A2
Pinchom's Hill Rd
DE56............... **3** A1
Pine Cl
Derby DE21........ **30** A4
Etwall DE65........ **58** C3
Pinecroft Ct DE21... **15** A1
Pines The DE72..... **41** A1
Pinewood Rd DE56 .. **2** A4
Pinfold The
Belper DE56........ **3** B3
Elvaston DE72...... **49** C4
Pingle DE22....... **12** A4
Pingle Cres DE56 ... **2** B3
Pinglehill Way
DE73.............. **48** B2
Pingle La DE56 ..... **2** B3
Pingle The
Derby DE21........ **31** B4
Melbourne DE73...**59** A2
Pingreaves Dr
DE73.............. **48** A2
Pintail Dr DE24.... **45** A4
Pippin Gdns DE24... **38** B3
Pit Close La DE73.... **48** A1
Pittar St DE22...... **61** A2
Plackett Cl DE72.... **41** C2
Plantain Gdns DE23. **35** B1
Platform Ct DE21 ... **30** C3
Playhouse Theatre★
DE1............... **61** C2
Plimsoll Ct DE21.... **61** A1
Plimsoll St DE22.... **17** B2
Ploughfield Cl
DE23.............. **35** A2
Plough Gate DE22 .. **12** B2
Plover Ct DE3 ..... **33** A3
Pollards Oaks DE72. **32** B1
Pond End DE74..... **53** B4
Pond Rd DE56 ...... **5** A1
Ponsonby Terr DE1 . **18** A1
Pontefract St DE24 . **37** C3
Pontypool Cl DE21.. **15** A2
Pool Cl DE24 ...... **48** C4
Poole St DE24...... **38** A2
Poplar Ave DE21.... **22** A1
Poplar Cl DE24 .... **39** A3
Poplar Nook DE22 .. **12** B4
Poplar Row DE22 ... **12** C1
Poplars The DE22 ... **12** B4
Porlock Ct DE21 .... **14** C2
Porter Pl DE21...... **21** C1
Porter Rd DE23 .... **27** B2
Porters La DE21.... **14** B3
Porter's La
Derby DE21........ **14** B3
Findern DE65 ...... **43** A1
Porthcawl Pl DE21.. **15** B2
Portico Rd DE22.... **34** C2
Portis Ct DE21...... **30** C3
Portland Cl DE3 .... **24** C2
Portland St
Derby DE23........ **36** C4
Etwall DE65....... **58** B3
Portman Chase
DE24.............. **45** A2

Portreath Dr DE22 .. **12** A3
Portway Cl DE22.... **12** C4
Portway Inf Sch
DE22............... **12** A4
Portway Jun Sch
DE22............... **12** A4
Posy La DE72...... **51** A2
Potter St
Derby DE21........ **30** C4
Melbourne DE73...**59** B2
Potters Yd DE73 .... **59** B2
Pottery Cl DE56..... **3** B3
Pottery Prim Sch
DE56.............. **3** B2
Powell St DE23 ..... **27** A2
Poyser Ave DE21.... **20** C3
Prescot Cl DE3 ..... **24** B1
Prestbury Cl DE22 .. **15** A1
Prestwick Way
DE73.............. **47** B2
Pride Park Stad
(Derby County FC)★
DE24.............. **29** A3
Pride Parkway
DE24.............. **28** C3
Pride Pl DE24...... **28** C3
Pride Point Dr
DE24.............. **28** C2
Priestland Ave
DE21.............. **30** C1
Primary Cl DE56 .... **2** C2
Prime Ind Est DE23 . **28** B2
Prime Ind Pk DE23 . **28** B2
Prime Parkway
DE1............... **60** C4
Primrose Bank
DE65.............. **58** C4
Primrose Cl DE21... **14** B3
Primula Way DE23 .. **45** A4
Prince Charles Ave
DE22.............. **16** C2
Princes Dr DE23 .... **26** A2
Princess Dr DE72 ... **31** C2
Prince's St DE23.... **28** A1
Priors Barn Cl
DE72.............. **32** C2
Priorway Ave DE72.. **32** C2
Priorway Gdns
DE72.............. **32** B1
Priory Cl DE73..... **50** C4
Priory Gdns DE21... **14** B3
Pritchett Dr DE23 .. **34** A4
Prospect Dr DE56... **4** A4
Prospect Pl DE24 ... **29** A4
Prospect Rd DE5 ... **6** B3
Provident St DE1 ... **27** C2
Pulborough Gdns
DE23.............. **34** C2
Pullman Rd DE21 ... **29** B4
Putney Cl DE22.... **16** A1
Pybus St DE22..... **17** C2
Pykestone Cl **6**
DE21.............. **14** B2
Pytchley Cl DE56... **3** C2

Q

Quaker Cl DE73.... **59** A2
Quantock Cl DE24 .. **45** A2
QUARNDON........ **8** B2
Quarndon Hts DE22. **11** B3
Quarndon View
DE22.............. **11** B2
Quarn Dr DE22..... **11** B2
Quarn Gdns DE1.... **18** B3
Quarn St DE1...... **18** A2
Quarn Way DE1.... **18** B2

Quarry Rd DE56..... **4** A4
Queen Mary Ct DE1. **18** B3
Queensbury Chase
DE23.............. **34** C2
Queens Ct
Derby DE22........ **18** A4
Draycott DE72..... **40** C1
Queens Dr DE23 ... **26** B2
Queen's Dr DE56 ... **2** A3
Queensferry Gdns
DE24.............. **47** B4
Queensgate Dr
DE73.............. **50** B4
Queensland Cl DE3 . **25** A4
Queen St
Belper DE56....... **2** C1
Derby DE1......... **60** B4
Queensway
Castle Donington
DE74.............. **52** C2
Derby DE22........ **12** B2
Melbourne DE73...**59** B3
Quick Cl DE73 ..... **59** A2
Quick Hill Rd DE24.. **45** A2
Quillings Way DE72 . **32** C1
Quintin Rd DE24 ... **38** C4
Quorn Rise DE23.... **36** A2

R

Rabown Ave DE23 .. **35** C4
Racecourse Ind Est
DE21.............. **19** B4
Radbourne La DE22. **16** A2
Radbourne St DE22. **17** B2
Radcliffe Ave DE21.. **20** B3
Radcliffe St DE23... **26** C3
Radford Mdw DE74 . **52** C1
Radford St DE24.... **38** B3
Radnor St DE21..... **19** C3
Radstock Gdns
DE21.............. **14** A1
Radstone Cl DE21... **15** A2
Raglan Ave DE22.... **17** B1
Railway Cotts DE24 . **36** C2
Railway Techical
Centre Bsns Pk
DE24.............. **28** C2
Railway Terr DE1.... **61** D2
Rainham Gdns
DE24.............. **38** C1
Rainier Dr DE21 .... **20** C2
Raleigh St DE22 .... **17** B2
Ramblers Dr DE21.. **15** B3
Ramsdean Cl DE21.. **19** C4
Ramshaw Way
DE22.............. **27** A4
Randolph Rd DE23.. **36** B4
Ranelagh Gdns
DE23.............. **17** A3
Rangemore Cl DE3 . **25** A4
Rannoch Cl
Derby DE22........ **12** A3
Derby, Spondon
DE21.............. **22** B1
Ranworth Cl DE24 .. **47** A3
Rauche Ct DE23 .... **61** C1
Raven Oak Cl DE56.. **2** C1
Ravenscourt Rd
DE22.............. **17** B2
Ravenscroft Dr
DE21.............. **20** B2
Ravensdale Inf & Jun
Schs DE21........**25** A3
Ravensdale Rd
DE22.............. **11** B3
Raven St DE22...... **27** A3
Rawdon St DE74.... **53** A2

Rawdon St DE23.... **27** B4
Rawlinson Ave
DE23.............. **36** C3
Rawson Gn DE56 ... **6** A3
RAWSON GREEN.... **6** A3
Raynesway
Derby, Alvaston
DE21.............. **39** A4
Derby DE21........ **29** C2
Raynesway Park Dr
DE21.............. **30** A1
Reader St DE21..... **22** A1
Realm Cl DE73...... **50** A4
Rebecca Ho DE1.... **18** A1
Rectory Gdns DE72 . **51** A2
Rectory La DE21.... **10** B1
Reculver Cl DE23 ... **35** C3
Redbury Cl DE21.... **27** A4
Redcar Gdns **6**
DE21.............. **13** C1
Redhill Ct DE56..... **4** C4
Redhill Foundation
Prim Sch DE72 ....**23** B1
Redland Cl DE24.... **45** C4
Redmires Dr DE73 .. **48** A2
Redruth Pl DE24 ... **39** B1
Redshaw St DE1.... **18** A3
Redstart Cl DE21.... **22** B2
Redway Croft **3**
DE73.............. **59** A3
Redwing Croft
DE23.............. **35** C3
Redwood Inf Sch
DE24.............. **45** C3
Redwood Jun Sch
DE24.............. **45** C3
Redwood Rd DE24.. **45** B3
Reeves Rd DE23 .... **28** A1
Regal Gate DE73.... **50** B4
Regency Cl DE23 ... **35** C3
Regent St DE1...... **61** C1
Reginald Rd N
DE21.............. **20** B3
Reginald Rd S DE21. **20** B2
Reginald St DE23 ... **28** A2
Regis Cl DE21...... **15** A2
Reigate Dr DE22.... **16** C3
Reigate Prim Sch
DE22.............. **16** B3
Renals St DE23..... **61** B1
Renfrew St DE21.... **20** A3
Repton Ave DE23 ... **26** C1
Retford Cl DE21.... **13** C2
Ribblesdale Cl
DE22.............. **11** B2
Richardson St
DE22.............. **17** C2
Richmond Ave
DE23.............. **35** B4
Richmond Cl DE23 . **34** C3
Richmond Dr DE56 . **7** A4
Richmond Rd
Derby, Chaddesden
DE21.............. **20** B2
Derby, Rose Hill
DE23.............. **27** C1
Riddings DE22...... **12** A4
Riddings St DE22 ... **27** B3
Ridgeway DE73..... **50** C4
Ridgeway Ave DE23. **35** C2
Ridgeway Cl DE23 .. **26** C2
Ridgeway Inf Sch
DE23.............. **35** C2
Ridgewood Ct
DE21.............. **14** A2
Ridings The DE72 ... **23** C1
Rigsby Ct DE3 ..... **24** B3
Rimsdale Cl DE24... **45** B3

Ringwood Cl **8**
DE21.............. **20** A4
Ripley Ho DE21..... **31** A3
Ripon Cres DE21.... **20** A4
Rise The DE22 ..... **12** A2
Risley La DE72..... **41** C4
Rivenhall Cl DE23... **34** B3
Rivermead Ho DE1.. **60** B5
Riverside Ct DE24... **28** C4
Riverside Rd DE23 .. **28** C4
River St DE1....... **60** B4
River View DE56 .... **4** A1
Robert St DE1...... **60** C4
Robin Croft Rd
DE22.............. **12** A4
Robinia Cl DE21.... **15** B3
Robin Rd DE1 ..... **18** B3
Robins Cl DE72 .... **39** C1
Robinscross DE72 .. **32** A1
Robinson Ind Est
DE23.............. **28** A2
Robson Ct DE24 .... **38** C3
Roby Lea DE74..... **52** C2
Rochester Cl DE24.. **38** C1
Rochley Cl DE21.... **14** B2
Rockbourne Cl
DE24.............. **39** C2
Rockhouse Rd
DE24.............. **38** C2
Rockingham Cl
DE22.............. **12** C4
Rodney Ho DE24.... **38** A2
Rodney Wlk DE23... **34** A3
Rodsley Cres DE23.. **35** C1
Roe Farm La DE21 .. **20** A3
Roe Farm Prim Sch
DE21.............. **20** A4
Roehampton Dr
DE22.............. **16** C3
Roe Wlk DE23..... **27** C1
Roman Rd DE1..... **19** A3
Roman Way DE72... **32** B1
Romsley Cl DE3.... **24** C4
Rona Cl DE24...... **45** B4
Ronald Cl DE23.... **34** A3
Roosevelt Ave
DE21.............. **21** A2
Rosamond's Ride
DE23.............. **35** C4
Rose Ave DE72..... **32** B1
Roseberry Ct DE21.. **15** A1
Rose Cl DE73 ..... **47** B1
Rosedale Ave DE23 . **38** C2
Roseheath Cl DE23 . **36** A1
ROSE HILL........ **28** A2
Rosehill Bsns Ctr
DE23.............. **27** C2
Rosehill Inf Sch
DE23.............. **28** A3
Rose Hill St DE23 ... **27** C2
Rosemary Dr DE24.. **38** C1
Rosemoor La DE21.. **15** A1
Rosemount Ct
DE22.............. **11** B3
Rosengrave St DE1 . **61** B2
Rosette Ct DE21 .... **15** B3
Rosewood Cl DE24.. **39** A3
Rossington Dr
DE23.............. **34** B2
Rosslyn Gdns DE24. **38** C2
Ross Wlk DE21..... **14** A1
Rosyth Cres DE73... **47** B1
Rothbury Pl DE21... **14** A1
Rothesay Cl DE24... **45** B4
Rothwell La DE56... **3** A2
Rothwell Rd DE3.... **24** C3
Rough Heanor Rd
DE3............... **25** C2

Roughton Cl DE3 . . . **33** C4
Roundhouse Rd
DE24 . . . . **28** B4
Routh Ave DE74 . . . . **56** B4
Rowallan Way DE73. **47** B1
Rowan Cl
Derby, Cherrytree Hill
DE21 . . . . **21** A1
Derby, Sinfin DE24 . . **45** A3
Rowan Dr DE56 . . . . . . **6** C2
Rowan Park Cl
DE23 . . . . **35** C3
Rowditch Ave DE22 . **26** C4
Rowditch Cotts
DE1 . . . . **26** C4
Rowditch Pl DE22. . . **26** C4
Rowena Cl DE24 . . . . **38** B3
Rowland St DE24 . . . . **38** A2
Rowley Gdns DE23 . . **35** B3
Rowley La DE23 . . . . . **35** B3
Rowleys Mill **5**
DE1 . . . . **18** A1
Rowsley Ave DE23 . . **35** C4
Roxburgh Ave DE21 **20** A3
Royal App DE73 . . . . **50** B4
Royal Cl DE72 . . . . . . **32** A1
Royal Crown Derby
Visitor Ctr * D23. . . **61** C1
Royal Gate DE56 . . . . . **3** C1
Royal Gr DE21 . . . . . **15** C3
Royal Hill Rd DE21 . **21** C2
Royal Sch for the Deaf
DE22 . . . . **17** C2
Royal Scot Rd DE24 **29** A2
Royal Way DE24 . . . . **29** A3
Roydon Cl DE3. . . . . . **24** B3
Royston Dr DE56 . . . . . **3** C3
Rudyard Ave DE21 . . **22** A2
Ruffstone Cl DE56 . . . **5** A1
Rugby St DE24. . . . . . **29** A1
Rupert Rd DE21 . . . . **20** C3
Rushcliffe Ave
DE21 . . . . **20** B2
Rushcliffe Gdns
DE21 . . . . **20** B2
Rushdale Ave DE23 . **35** C2
Rushup Cl DE22 . . . . . **9** B1
Ruskin Rd DE1. . . . . . **18** B3
Ruskin Way DE23 . . . **35** A4
Russell St DE24. . . . . **28** B1
Russet Cl DE21 . . . . . **15** A1
Russet Ct DE23 . . . . . **27** A2
Rutherford Rise **8**
DE21 . . . . **14** B2
Rutland Ave DE72. . . **32** B2
Rutland Dr DE3 . . . . . **25** A3
Rutland St DE23 . . . . **27** C1
Ryal Cl DE72. . . . . . . **23** B1
Ryan Cl DE24 . . . . . . **45** B3
Rydal Cl DE22 . . . . . . **12** A4
Ryde Ho DE24 . . . . . . **39** B3
Rye Butts DE73 . . . . **47** C1
Rye Cl DE21 . . . . **14** A3
Ryedale Gdns DE23 . **35** B1
Ryegrass Cl DE56 . . . . **3** C2
Ryegrass Rd DE21 . . **15** B2
Rykneld Cl DE23 . . . . **34** A2
Rykneld Dr DE23. . . . **34** B3
Rykneld Rd DE23 . . . **34** A2
Rykneld Way DE23 . . **34** A2
Rykneld Hill DE5 . . . . **6** C4
Rykneld Rd DE56,
DE7 . . . . **6** C2
Rymill Dr DE21 . . . . **14** B1

S

Sacheverel St DE1 . . **61** B2
Sackville St DE23 . . . **36** B4
Saddleworth Wlk
DE24 . . . . **47** B3
Sadler Gate DE1 . . . . **60** B3
Saffron Dr DE21 . . . . **14** C1
St Agnes Ave DE22 . . **11** C4
St Alban's RC Prim Sch
DE21 . . . . **20** B2
St Albans Rd DE22 . . **26** C3
St Alkmund's Cl
DE56 . . . . **7** B3
St Alkmunds Way
DE56 . . . . **7** B3
St Alkmund's Way
DE1 . . . . **60** B4
St Andrews Sch
DE21 . . . . **14** A1
St Andrews View
DE21 . . . . **14** A1
St Anne's Cl DE1. . . . **18** A2
St Anne's La DE74 . . **53** B1
St Augustine St
DE23 . . . . **27** B1
St Benedict RC Sch &
Performing Arts Coll
DE22 . . . . **12** A1
St Bride's Wlk DE22 **17** A2
St Chad's CE Inf Sch
DE23 . . . . **27** B2
St Chad's Cl DE72. . . **40** C1
St Chad's Rd DE23 . . **27** B2
St Christopher's Way
DE24 . . . . **28** C3
St Clare's Cl DE22 . . **26** C2
St Clare's Sch DE23 . **25** C2
St Cuthbert's Rd
DE22 . . . . **26** B3
St David's Cl DE22 . . **26** C3
St Edmund's Cl
DE22 . . . . **12** B4
St Edward's CE Prim
Sch DE74 . . . . **53** B1
St Edward's Rd
DE74 . . . . **56** B4
St Elizabeth's RC Prim
Sch DE56 . . . . **2** B3
St George's Cl DE22. **12** B3
St George's Ho
DE22 . . . . **12** B3
St George's Pl **1**
DE56 . . . . **2** B2
St George's RC Prim
Sch DE23 . . . . **35** B3
St Giles Rd DE23 . . . **27** B1
St Giles Sch DE21 . . . **13** B1
St Helen's St DE1. . . **60** B4
St Hugh's Cl DE22 . . **12** C2
St James' CE Inf Sch
DE23 . . . . **61** C1
St Jame's CE Jun Sch
DE23 . . . . **28** A3
St James Cl DE56 . . . . **3** C2
St James' Rd DE23 . . **27** B1
St James' St
Derby DE1. . . . . **60** B3
Derby, Rose Hill
DE23 . . . . **27** C1
St John Fisher RC
Prim Sch DE24 . . . . **39** B4
St John's Ave DE21 . **21** A1
St John's CE Prim Sch
DE56 . . . . **3** A3
St John's Cl DE22 . . . **11** C3
St John's Dr
Derby DE21. . . . . **21** A1

St John's Dr continued
Kilburn DE56. . . . . **6** B2
St John's Rd DE56 . . . **2** C2
St John's Terr DE1 . . **18** B2
St Joseph's RC Prim
Sch DE23 . . . . **61** A1
St Katherine's Ct
DE22 . . . . **17** C2
St Laurence Gdns **10**
DE56 . . . . **2** B2
ST LUKE'S **27** A3
St Mark's Rd DE21 . . **19** C2
St Martin's Sch
DE24 . . . . **38** B4
St Mary's Ave DE72 . **40** C1
St Mary's Cl DE24. . . **38** C2
St Mary's Ct DE1. . . . **60** B4
St Mary's Gate DE1 . **60** B3
St Mary's RC Prim Sch
DE22 . . . . **12** B1
St Mary's RC Prim Sch
DE1 . . . . **60** B4
St Marys Wharf Rd
DE1 . . . . **19** A3
St Matthew's Wlk **4**
DE22 . . . . **12** B2
St Mawes Cl DE22 . . **11** C4
St Mellion Cl DE3 . . . **21** B1
St Michaels Cl
DE24 . . . . **39** B3
St Michael's Cl DE56 . **5** A1
St Michael's La DE1 . **60** B4
St Michaels View
DE24 . . . . **39** B3
St Nicholas Cl
DE22 . . . . **11** C2
St Nicholas Pl DE1. . **60** A5
St Pancras Way
DE1 . . . . **60** C5
St Paul's Rd DE1. . . . **18** C3
St Peter's CE Jun Sch
DE23 . . . . **26** B1
St Peter's Churchyard
DE1 . . . . **60** B3
St Peter's Cl **8** DE56. **2** B2
St Peters Croft DE56 . **2** C2
St Peters Ct DE24 . . . **38** C4
St Peter's Rd DE73. . **48** A1
St Peter's St DE1 . . . **61** B3
St Peter's Way DE1 . **61** B2
St Quentin Cl DE22 . **26** B3
St Ronan's Ave DE56 . **7** B1
St Stephens Cl
DE72 . . . . **32** A1
St Stephen's Cl
DE23 . . . . **35** C2
St Swithin's Cl
DE22 . . . . **26** C3
St Swithuns Ct DE56 . **4** B4
St Thomas Rd DE23 . **27** C1
St Werburgh's CE Prim
Sch DE21. . . . . **21** C1
St Werburgh's View
DE21 . . . . **21** C1
St Wystan's Rd
DE22 . . . . **26** B3
Sale St DE23. . . . . . . **28** A2
Salisbury Dr DE56 . . . **3** C3
Salisbury La DE73 . . **59** B2
Salisbury St DE23 . . **61** B1
Sallywood Cl DE24 . . **45** A2
Saltburn Cl DE21 . . . **13** B1
Salter Cl DE74 . . . . . **52** C2
Samantha Ct DE21. . **15** A1
Sancroft Ave DE21 . . **22** A2
Sancroft Rd DE21. . . **22** B2
Sandalwood Cl
DE24 . . . . **39** B3

Sandbach Cl DE21 . . **14** C1
Sandbed La DE56 . . . . **5** A4
Sanderling Heath
DE3 . . . . **33** A3
Sanderson Rd DE21 **21** A2
Sandfield Cl DE21. . . **21** A4
Sandgate Cl DE24 . . **38** C2
Sandown Ave DE3 . . **24** B3
Sandown Rd DE24 . . **38** A4
Sandpiper La DE3 . . **33** A2
Sandringham Dr
DE21 . . . . **22** B1
Sandringham Ho
DE24 . . . . **28** C1
Sandringham Rd
DE21 . . . . **14** A1
Sandyhill Cl DE23. . . **48** A2
Santolina Dr DE21 . . **14** B1
Sapperton Cl DE23. . **35** C1
Sapphire Dr DE5. . . . . **6** C4
Saundersfoot Way
DE21 . . . . **15** B2
Sawley Rd DE72 . . . . **41** A1
Saxondale Ave DE3 . **24** B4
Scarborough Rise
DE21 . . . . **13** C1
Scarcliffe Cl DE24 . . **47** B3
Scarsdale Ave
Derby, Allestree
DE22 . . . . **11** C3
Derby, Littleover
DE23 . . . . **26** B2
Scarsdale Rd DE56. . . **7** B2
Sch of Nursing (Univ
of Nottingham)
DE1 . . . . **61** C2
School La
Castle Donington
DE74 . . . . **53** A2
Chellaston DE73. . . . **48** A2
School Yd The DE1. . **60** B4
Scotches The DE56 . . **2** B3
Scott Dr DE56 . . . . **3** D3
Scott St DE23 . . . . . . **27** B1
Scropton Wlk DE24 . **47** B3
Seagrave Cl DE21. . . **21** A4
Seale St DE1 . . . . **60** B5
Searl St DE1 . . . . **18** B2
Seascale Cl **5**
DE21 . . . . **13** C1
Seaton Cl DE3 . . . . . . **24** B3
Second Ave DE73 . . . **50** C4
Sedgebrook Cl **2**
DE21 . . . . **14** B2
Sedgefield Gn DE3. . **24** B1
Sedgemoor Way
DE23 . . . . **34** C1
Sefton Rd DE21. . . . . **20** B2
Sefton Way DE56 . . . . **7** A3
Selborne St DE24 . . . **28** C2
Selina Cl DE74. . . . . . **53** A2
Selina St DE73. . . . . . **59** A2
Selkirk St DE21 . . . . **20** A3
Selworthy Cl DE21 . . **14** C2
Selwyn St DE22. . . . . **17** B2
Serina Ave DE23 . . . **35** C4
Settlement The
DE72 . . . . **23** B1
Sevenlands Dr
DE24 . . . . **48** C4
Sevenoaks Ave
DE22 . . . . **16** B2
Severnale Cl DE22 . . . **9** C1
Severn St DE24. . . . . **38** B4
Seymour Cl DE21 . . . **17** B1
SHACKLECROSS . . . **32** C1
Shacklecross Cl
DE72 . . . . **32** B1

Rou–Shr **75**

Shaftesbury Cres
DE23 . . . . **28** A1
Shaftesbury St S
DE23 . . . . **28** A1
Shaftesbury St
DE23 . . . . **28** A2
Shakespeare St
DE24 . . . . **36** C1
Shaldon Dr DE23 . . . **26** C1
Shalfleet Dr DE24. . . **39** B1
Shamrock St DE23 . . **27** A1
Shandwick Ct **10**
DE24 . . . . **45** A3
Shanklin Ho DE24. . . **39** B3
Shannon Cl DE23 . . . **35** C2
Shannon Ho DE24 . . **38** A1
Shannon Sq DE21 . . **30** A4
Shardlow Rd
Aston-on-T DE72. . . . **51** B2
Derby DE24, DE74 . . **39** B2
Shaw La DE56 . . . . **4** C1
Shaws Gn DE22 . . . . **17** C2
Shaw St DE22 . . . . . . **18** A2
Shaw's Yd DE56. . . . . **6** A2
Shearwater Cl
DE23 . . . . **35** C3
Sheffield Pl DE1 . . . . **61** D2
Sheldon Cl DE24. . . . **47** B3
Shelford Cl DE3 . . . . **24** B3
Shelley Dr DE24 . . . . **36** C1
Shelmory Cl DE24 . . **38** A1
Shelton Dr DE24 . . . . **47** C3
Shelton Gate Cl
DE24 . . . . **38** A1
Shelton Jun & Inf Schs
DE24 . . . . **47** A4
SHELTON LOCK **47** C3
Shenington Way
DE21 . . . . **15** A2
Shepherd St DE23 . . **27** B1
Sherbourne Dr DE56. **3** C3
Sheridan St DE24 . . . **36** B1
Sherroside Cl DE22 . **11** C4
Sherston Cl DE21 . . . **15** A2
Sherwin St DE22. . . . **18** A4
Sherwood Ave
Borrowash DE72. . . . **32** C2
Derby, Chaddesden
DE21 . . . . **20** B3
Derby, Littleover
DE23 . . . . **35** C1
Sherwood St DE22. . **27** A3
Shetland Cl DE11 . . . **19** B3
Shields Cres DE74 . . **52** C1
Shipley Wlk DE24 . . **47** B3
Shiregate Gdns
DE23 . . . . **34** C1
Shireoaks Cl DE56 . . . **2** A3
Shireoaks Ct DE23 . . **35** B3
Shirland Ct DE24 . . . **47** B3
Shirley Cl DE74. . . . . **53** A2
Shirley Cres DE72. . . **41** C2
Shirley Pk DE72. . . . . **51** B2
Shirley Rd DE21 . . . . **14** B1
Shop Stones DE72 . . **23** B1
Short Ave DE22 . . . . . . **9** A1
Short La DE74 . . . . . . **52** C2
Short Lands DE56. . . . **2** C2
Short Row **4** DE56 . . **2** B2
Short St DE56 . . . . **3** A2
Shorwell Gdns
DE24 . . . . **39** B1
Shottle Wlk DE24 . . . **47** B3
Shrewsbury Cl
DE21 . . . . **15** B2

Shropshire Ave
DE21 . . . . 20 A3
Siddals La DE22 . . . . 12 B4
Siddals Rd DE1 . . . . . 61 C2
Siddons St DE24 . . . . 38 C3
Sidings The DE21 . . . 29 C4
Sidmouth Cl DE24 . . 39 B3
Sidney Robinson Bsns
Pk DE24 . . . . 28 C3
Sidney St DE1 . . . . . . 28 A3
Silk Mill La DE1 . . . 60 B4
Silk Mill The* DE1 . 60 B4
Silverburn Dr DE21 . 14 C2
Silverdale Cl DE73 . . 48 A2
Silverhill Prim Sch
DE3 . . . . 24 B3
Silverhill Rd DE21 . . 31 A3
Silver Hill Rd DE23. . 27 C2
Silverton Dr DE24. . . 44 C2
Silvey Gr DE21 . . . . 30 C4
Simcoe Leys DE73 . . 48 A2
Sims Ave DE1. . . . . . 18 A1
Sinclair Cl DE24 . . . 45 B4
SINFIN 45 C4
Sinfin Ave DE24. . . . 47 A3
Sinfin Central Bsns Pk
DE23, DE24. . . . . 36 B1
Sinfin Com Sch
DE24 . . . . 45 B3
Sinfin District Ctr
DE24 . . . . 45 B3
Sinfin Fields Cres
DE24 . . . . 37 C1
Sinfin La DE23,
DE24 . . . . 45 C4
Sinfin Moor La
DE73 . . . . 47 B2
Sinfin Prim Sch
DE24 . . . . 36 B1
Sir Francis Ley Ind Pk
DE23 . . . . 28 B1
Sir Frank Whittle Rd
DE21 . . . . 19 B3
Siskin Cl DE3 . . . . . . 33 A3
Siskin Dr DE24. . . . . 45 A4
Sister's La DE27 . . . 23 B1
Sitwell Cl DE21 . . . . 30 C4
Sitwell Dr DE56. . . . . 6 B2
Sitwell St
Derby DE1. . . . . 61 B2
Derby, Spondon
DE21 . . . . 31 A4
Skiddaw Dr DE3 . . . 25 A1
Skipness Cl DE73 . . 47 B2
Skipton Gn DE21. . . 13 B1
Skylark Way DE24 . . 45 A4
Slack La
Derby, Allestree
DE22 . . . . 12 B2
Derby, New Zealand
DE22 . . . . 17 C1
Slade DE65 . . . . . . 58 C3
Slade La DE73, DE74 54 A1
Slade Lands Dr
DE73 . . . . 48 A2
Slaidburn Cl DE3 . . 25 A1
Slaney Cl DE24 . . . . 38 A3
Slater Ave DE22 . . . 18 A2
Sledmere Cl DE24 . . 39 B3
Sleepy La DE73 . . . . 59 C4
Slindon Croft DE24 . 39 C2
Sloane Rd DE22 . . . 16 C2
Smalley Dr DE21. . . 15 A3
Small Meer Cl
DE73 . . . . 47 C1

Smisby Way DE24. . . 47 B3
Smith Ave DE73. . . . 59 B4
Snake La DE56. . . . . . 7 B3
Snelsmoor La DE73 . 48 B2
Snelston Cres DE23 26 C2
Snowberry Ave DE56. 3 A1
Society Pl DE23 . . . . 27 C2
Solway Cl DE21. . . . 14 C2
Somerby Way 3
DE21 . . . . 14 B2
Somersal Cl DE24. . . 47 B3
Somerset St DE21 . . 19 C3
Somme Rd DE22. . . . 11 A3
South Ave
Chellaston DE73 . . . . 47 C3
Derby, Darley Abbey
DE22 . . . . 12 C2
Derby DE23. . . . . 26 C1
Derby, Spondon
DE21 . . . . 31 A4
South Brae Cl DE23 35 C3
Southcroft DE23. . . . 45 A4
Southdown Cl
DE24. . . . . 44 C2
South Dr
Chellaston DE73 . . . . 47 C3
Derby, Cherrytree Hill
DE21 . . . . 20 C1
Derby, Litteover DE3. . 18 B3
Southgate Bsns Ctr
DE23 . . . . 61 B1
Southgate Cl DE3. . . 24 B3
Southmead Way
DE3 . . . . 26 A3
South St
Derby DE1. . . . . 18 A1
Draycott DE72 . . . . . . 40 C1
Melbourne DE73 . . . . 59 A2
South View DE23. . . . 26 B1
Southwark Cl DE22 . 17 A1
Southwood St DE24. 38 B4
Sovereign Way
DE21 . . . . 15 C3
Sowter Rd DE1 . . . . . 60 B4
Spa Ct DE1 . . . . 61 A1
Spa La DE1 . . . . 61 A1
Sparrow Cl DE24. . . . 45 A4
Speedwell Cl DE21. . 15 B3
Spenbeck Dr DE22. . . 9 B1
Spencer Ave
Belper DE56 . . . . 3 A2
Derby DE24. . . . . 47 A4
Spencer Ho
Derby, Crewton
DE24 . . . . 38 C4
Derby, Spondon
DE21 . . . . 30 C3
Spencer Rd DE56 . . . 3 A2
Spencer St DE24. . . 38 C4
Spindletree Dr
DE21 . . . . 14 B2
Spinners Way DE56 . . 3 B3
Spinneybrook Way
DE3 . . . . 24 C4
Spinney Cl DE22 . . . 12 C2
Spinney Hill DE73. . 59 A2
Spinney The
Derby, Chaddesden
DE21 . . . . 20 B3
Derby DE22. . . . . 27 A3
Spinney The
Belper DE56 . . . . 2 C4
Borrowash DE72. . . . . 32 B1
Castle Donington
DE74 . . . . 53 A2
Spittal DE74. . . . . . . 53 A2
Spittal Hill DE74. . . 53 A2
SPONDON 31 A4

Spondon Sch DE21 . 30 B4
Spondon Sta DE21. . 30 C3
Spooney Wood Ct
DE23 . . . . 34 B3
Spring Cl
Belper DE56 . . . . 2 A4
Breaston DE72 . . . . . 41 B2
Springdale Ct DE3 . . 25 A1
Springfield DE3 . . . . 26 A2
Springfield Dr DE56. . 7 A2
Springfield Prim Sch
DE21 . . . . 21 C1
Springfield Rd
Chellaston DE73 . . . . 47 C2
Derby, Cherrytree Hill
DE21 . . . . 21 A1
Etwall DE65 . . . . 58 B2
Spring Gdns DE21 . . 20 B3
Spring St DE22 . . . . 61 A2
Springwood Dr
DE21 . . . . 15 A2
Springwood Gdns
DE56 . . . . 2 C2
Square The
Derby, Darley Abbey
DE22 . . . . 12 C1
Derby DE3. . . . . 24 C1
Squires Way DE23 . . 34 C2
Stables St DE22. . . . 17 C1
Stadium Bsns Ct
DE24 . . . . 29 A4
Stadium View DE24 . 29 A3
Stadmoor Ct DE73 . . 47 C1
Stafford Ho DE24 . . 38 A2
Stafford St DE1 . . . . 60 A3
Staines Cl DE3. . . . . 24 B2
Staithes Wlk DE21. . 13 B1
Staker La DE3 . . . . . 33 C2
Stamford St DE24. . . 37 C2
Stanage Gn DE3 . . . 25 B1
Stanhope Rd DE3 . . 25 A3
Stanhope St DE23 . . 27 C2
Stanier Way DE21. . . 29 C3
Stanley Cl DE22. . . . 18 B4
Stanley Rd
Derby, Allenton
DE24 . . . . 38 B2
Derby, Cherrytree Hill
DE21 . . . . 20 C1
Stanley St DE22. . . . 17 C1
Stanstead Rd DE3 . . 24 B3
Stanton Ave DE56. . . 3 A2
Stanton St DE23 . . . 27 B1
Starcross Ct DE3. . . 24 B3
Starkie Ave DE74 . . 52 C1
Statham St DE22. . . 18 A3
Station App
Derby DE1. . . . . 60 B4
Duffield DE56 . . . . 7 C3
Station Cl
Chellaston DE73 . . . . 47 C1
Kilburn DE56 . . . . 6 A3
Station Rd
Borrowash DE72. . . . . 32 A1
Breadsall DE21. . . . . 14 A4
Castle Donington
DE74 . . . . 53 C3
Chellaston DE73 . . . . 47 C1
Derby DE3. . . . . 24 C1
Derby, Spondon
DE21 . . . . 30 C3
Draycott DE72 . . . . . . 41 A1
Duffield DE56 . . . . 7 C3
Little Eaton DE21 . . . 10 A3
Melbourne DE73 . . . . 59 C3
Station Yd DE73 . . . . 59 C3
Staunton Ave DE23 . 36 A2
Staunton Cl DE74. . . 53 A2

Staveley Cl DE24. . . . 47 B3
Staverton Dr DE3 . . 24 C4
Steeple Cl DE21 . . . . 14 A2
Stenson Ave DE23 . . 36 A2
Stenson Rd DE23, DE24. . 45 A2
Stenson Rd DE23,
DE24. . . . . 45 A4
Stephensons Way
DE21 . . . . 29 C3
Stepping Cl DE22 . . 18 A1
Stepping La DE22. . . 18 A1
Sterling Cl DE5 . . . . . 6 C4
Sterndale Ho 4
DE1. . . . . 61 B2
Stevenage Cl DE24. . 38 B1
Stevens La DE72 . . . 41 C2
Stevenson Ave
DE72. . . . . 41 A1
Stevenson Pl DE23. . 35 A4
Stewart Cl DE21 . . . . 22 A2
Stiles Rd DE24. . . . . 39 A4
Stirling Cl DE21. . . . 19 B4
Stockbrook Rd
DE22 . . . . 26 C3
Stockbrook St
DE22 . . . . 27 A4
Stockdove Cl DE24. . 45 A4
Stocker Ave DE24 . . 39 C3
Stoke Cl DE56 . . . . . . 3 D3
Stonebroom Wlk
DE24 . . . . 47 B3
Stonechat Cl DE3. . . 25 C3
Stone Cl DE21 . . . . . 22 A2
Stonehill Rd DE24. . 56 B4
Stone Hill Rd DE23 . 27 B2
Stonesby Cl DE21. . . 14 B2
Stonesdale Ct 1
DE24 . . . . 39 B2
Stoney Cross DE21. . 31 A3
Stoneyfield Bank
DE56 . . . . 2 C3
Stoney Flatts Cres
DE21 . . . . 20 C3
Stoney Gate Rd
DE21 . . . . 30 C3
Stoney La DE21. . . . 22 A1
Stonyhurst Ct DE24 . 47 B3
Stoodley Pike Gdns
DE22 . . . . 11 B2
Stores Rd DE21 . . . . 60 D4
Stornoway Cl 9
DE24 . . . . 45 A3
Stourport Dr DE3 . . 48 A3
Stowmarket Dr
DE21 . . . . 19 C4
Strand DE1. . . . . 60 B3
Strand Arc DE1. . . . . 60 B3
Stratford Rd DE21 . . 13 C2
Strathaven Ct DE21. 22 A1
Strathmore Ave
DE24 . . . . 38 C2
Streatham Rd DE22 . 17 A2
Stretton Cl DE3. . . . 24 C1
Stroma Cl DE24. . . . 45 C4
Strutt's Park Ho 2
DE22 . . . . 18 B3
Strutt St
Belper DE56 . . . . 2 B1
Derby DE23. . . . . 27 C2
Stuart St DE1. . . . . . 60 B4
Studbrook Cl DE74 . 52 C1
Sturges La DE72 . . . 49 C4
Sudbury Cl DE1. . . . 18 A1
Sudbury St DE1. . . . 18 A1
Suffolk Ave DE21 . . 20 A3
Sulleys Field DE22 . . 8 B3

Summerbrook Ct
DE22 . . . . 27 B4
Summerville Cl
DE23 . . . . 35 A2
Summer Wood Ct
DE23 . . . . 35 C3
Sunart Cl DE24 . . . . 45 C2
Sundew Cl DE21. . . . 31 B4
Sundown Ave DE23 . 35 C2
Sunflower Cl DE24. . 29 C1
Sunningdale Ave
DE21 . . . . 21 C1
Sunny Bank Gdns
DE56 . . . . 4 A4
Sunny Gr DE21 . . . . 20 C1
SUNNY HILL 35 C3
Sunny Hill DE56 . . . . 4 A1
Sunnyhill Ave DE23 . 36 A2
Sunnyhill Inf Sch
DE23 . . . . 36 A3
Sun St DE22 . . . . . . 61 A2
Surbiton Cl DE22 . . 16 C2
Surrey St DE22 . . . . 17 C2
Sussex Cir DE21 . . . 20 A4
Sutherland Rd
DE23 . . . . 27 C1
Sutton Ave DE73 . . . 47 C3
Sutton Cl DE21 . . . . 17 C2
Sutton Dr DE24 . . . . 47 B4
Sutton Ho DE24. . . . 39 B1
Sutton La DE65 . . . . 58 B4
Swaledale Ct 2
DE24 . . . . 39 B2
Swallow Cl DE3. . . . 25 C3
Swallowdale Rd
DE24. . . . . 45 A4
Swallow Ho DE1. . . . 18 A1
Swan Hill DE3 . . . . 33 A2
Swanmore Rd DE23 34 C4
Swanwick Gdns
DE21 . . . . 14 C1
Swarkestone Dr
DE23 . . . . 35 B1
Swarkestone Rd
DE73 . . . . 50 B4
Swayfield Cl DE3 . . 24 B3
Sweetbriar Cl DE24 38 C1
Swift Cl DE23 . . . . . 25 C3
Swinburne St DE1 . . 61 B1
Swinderby Dr DE21 . 15 A1
Swinney Bank DE56. . 2 C3
Swinney La DE56 . . . 2 C3
Swinscoe Ho 3
DE1 . . . . 61 B2
Sycamore Ave
Derby DE22. . . . . 11 C3
Findern DE65 . . . . . . 43 B1
Sycamore Cl DE65 . . 58 C3
Sycamore Ct DE21 . . 22 A1
Sycamore Rd DE74. . 53 B3
Sydenham Rd DE22 16 C3
Sydney Cl DE3 . . . . 25 B3
Sydney Rd DE72 . . . 40 C1

T

Taddington Cl 2
DE21. . . . . 20 A4
Taddington Rd
DE21 . . . . 14 B1
Talbot St DE1. . . . . . 61 A3
Talgarth Cl DE21. . . 15 B2
Tamar Ave DE22 . . . 11 C4
Tamworth Rise DE56. 7 B2
Tamworth St DE56 . . 7 B2
Tamworth Terr DE56 . 7 B3
Tansley Rise 4
DE21 . . . . 14 B1

Tanyard Cl DE74 . . . . 53 B2
Taplow Cl DE3 . . . . . 24 B2
Tarina Cl DE3 . . . . . . 48 A1
Tasman Cl DE3 . . . . . 25 B3
Taunton Cl DE24 . . . . 39 B4
Taverners Cres
DE23 . . . . 35 B4
Tavistock Cl 14
DE24 . . . . 45 A3
Tawny Way DE23. . . 34 C3
Tayberry Cl DE24 . . 38 A3
Tay Cl DE24 . . . . 45 A2
Taylor St DE24 . . . . 29 A2
Tayside DE24 . . . . . 45 A3
Tay Wlk DE24 . . . . . 12 A3
Tedworth Ave DE24. 45 A2
Telford Cl DE3 . . . . . 25 A1
Templar Cl DE24 . . . 44 C3
Templebell Cl DE23 34 C2
Temple St DE23 . . . . 27 C3
Tenant St DE1 . . . . . 60 B3
Tenby Dr DE21. . . . . 15 B2
Tennessee Rd DE21 21 A3
Tennyson St DE24 . . 37 C3
Terr The DE21 . . . . . . 20 A3
Terry Pl DE24 . . . . . . 38 B2
Teviot Pl DE21 . . . . . 14 C2
Tewkesbury Cres
DE21 . . . . 19 C4
Thackeray St DE24. . 36 C1
Thames Cl DE22 . . . . 16 B1
Thanet Dr DE24. . . . 38 C2
Thatch Cl DE22 . . . . 12 B2
Theatre Wlk DE1 . . . 61 C3
THE GUTTER 3 B2
Thirlmere Ave
DE22 . . . . 12 A3
Thirsk Pl DE24 . . . . 37 C3
Thistledown Cl
DE22 . . . . 12 C2
Thistle Gr DE73 . . . . 47 B1
Thomas Cook Cl
DE73 . . . . 59 A2
Thomas St DE1 . . . . 27 A4
Thoresby Cl DE21. . . 15 A1
Thoresby Cres
DE72 . . . . 40 B1
Thorn Cl DE22 . . . . . 11 C4
Thorndike Ave
DE24 . . . . 38 C3
Thorndon Cl DE3 . . . 33 C4
Thorness Cl DE24 . . 39 B1
Thornhill Rd DE23 . . 26 B1
Thorn St DE23 . . . . . 27 B2
Thorntree La DE1. . . 60 B3
Thorpe Dr DE3 . . . . 25 A3
Thorpelands Dr
DE22 . . . . 12 A1
Thorpe Way DE56. . . 3 A3
Three Gates DE24 . . . 4 A4
Thrushton Cl DE65. . 42 C2
Thruxton Cl DE24 . . 39 B2
THULSTON 49 C4
Thurlow Ct DE21. . . 14 C1
Thurrows Way
DE73. . . . . 48 B2
Thurstone Furlong
DE73. . . . . 47 B1
Thyme Cl DE23 . . . . 45 A4
Tiber Cl DE24 . . . . . 39 C1
Tickham Ave DE24. . 44 C2
Ticknall La DE5, DE6 . 6 C3
Ticknall Wlk DE23 . . 36 A4
Tideswell Rd DE21. . 14 B1
Tilbury Pl DE24 . . . . 38 C1
Tiller Cl DE23 . . . . . 35 A2
Timbersbrook Cl
DE21 . . . . 14 C1

Timsbury Ct DE21. . . 14 A2
Tintagel Cl 2 DE23 . 28 A2
Tipnall Rd DE74 . . . . 53 A1
Tiree Cl DE24 . . . . . . 45 C4
Tissington Dr DE21 . 15 B3
Tiverton Cl DE3 . . . . 24 C4
Tivoli Gdns DE1 . . . . 18 A3
Tobermory Way
DE24 . . . . 45 A3
Tomlinson Ct DE24. . 38 B3
Tomlinson Ind Est
DE21 . . . . 13 B2
Tomlinsons Cotts
DE21 . . . . 13 B2
Tonbridge Dr DE24 . 38 C1
Top Farm Ct DE56. . . 6 A2
Topley Gdns DE21. . 14 B2
Top Manor Cl DE72 . 23 B1
Torridon Cl DE24 . . . 45 B4
Touchstone Ct
DE73 . . . . 47 A2
Tower St DE24 . . . . . 37 C3
Towle Cl DE72 . . . . . 32 B1
Towles Pastures
DE74 . . . . 53 A1
Town End Rd DE72. . 41 A1
Townsend Gr DE73. . 48 A2
Town St
Duffield DE56 . . . . . . 7 C2
Holbrook DE56 . . . . . 5 A1
Town The DE21 . . . . 10 A3
Traffic St DE1. . . . . . 61 C2
Trafford Way DE23 . . 35 B4
Tredegar Dr DE21. . . 15 A2
Trefoil Ct DE23 . . . . 34 C3
Tregaron Cl DE21 . . 15 B2
Tregony Way DE24 . . 45 A3
Trent Bridge Ct
DE23 . . . . 35 B4
Trent Cl DE24 . . . . . . 45 A2
Trent Dr DE23 . . . . . 35 C2
Trent La
Castle Donington
DE74 . . . . 53 A3
King's Newton DE73. . 59 C4
Trent Lane Ind Est
DE74 . . . . 53 B3
Trenton Gn DE21. . . 21 A2
Trenton Green Dr
DE21 . . . . 21 A2
Trent Rise DE21. . . . 31 B4
Trent St DE24 . . . . . 38 C3
Tresillian Cl DE22 . . 12 A2
Treveris Cl DE21 . . . 31 A4
Trevone Cl DE24 . . . 39 B1
Triangle The DE56. . . 2 B2
Trinity St DE1 . . . . . 61 C2
Trocadero Ct DE23. . 61 B1
Troon Cl DE23 . . . . . 34 C4
Troutbeck Cl DE22 . 33 C3
Trowbridge Cl
DE21 . . . . 14 A2
Trowels La DE22 . . . 26 B4
Truro Cres DE21 . . . 20 A4
Trusley Gdns DE23 . 35 C1
Tudor Ct 3 DE22 . 12 B3
Tudor Field Cl
DE73 . . . . 48 A1
Tudor Rd DE21. . . . . 20 C2
Tuffield Gdns DE22 . 17 A3
Tulla Cl DE24 . . . . . 45 B2
Tuphall Cl DE73. . . . 48 B2
Turner's Almshouses
DE22. . . . . 17 C2
Turner St DE24 . . . . 38 A2
Tuxford Cl DE21 . . . 15 A1
Tweeds Muir Cl 5
DE21 . . . . 14 B2

Twickenham Dr
DE22 . . . . 16 C2
Twin Oaks Cl DE23 . . 34 B3
Twyford St DE23 . . . 61 B1
Tyndale Chase
DE24 . . . . 44 C2
Tynefield Ct DE65. . . 58 B1
Tynefield Mews
DE65. . . . . 58 B1

U

Uffa Magna DE3 . . . 24 B1
Ullswater Cl DE21. . 13 C2
Ullswater Dr DE21 . 22 A1
Underhill Ave DE23 . 36 B3
Underhill Cl DE23. . 36 A2
Underpass The DE1 . 60 C4
Union St DE73 . . . . . 59 A2
Univ of Derby DE22 11 C1
Univ of Derby (Green
Lane Campus)
DE1 . . . . 61 B2
Univ of Derby (Sch of
Health & Com
Studies) DE23 . . . . 26 C2
Upchurch Cl DE3 . . 24 B3
Uplands Ave DE23 . . 35 B2
Uplands Gdns DE23 27 A2
Upper Bainbrigge St
DE23 . . . . 27 C3
Upper Boundary Rd
DE22 . . . . 27 A4
Upper Dale Rd
DE23 . . . . 27 B1
Upper Hall Cl DE56 . . 5 A1
Upper Hollow DE56 . 26 B1
Upper Moor Rd
DE24 . . . . 38 A2
Upton Cl DE74. . . . . 53 B2
Uttoxeter New Rd
DE22 . . . . 26 B3
Uttoxeter Old Rd
DE22 . . . . 18 A1
Uttoxeter Rd DE3 . . 25 A1

V

Vale Mills DE22 . . . . 27 B3
Valerie Rd DE72 . . . . 51 A2
Valley Rd
Derby, Cherrytree Hill
DE21 . . . . 21 A1
Derby DE23. . . . . . . 26 C1
Valley View DE56. . . . 4 B4
Vancouver Ave
DE21 . . . . 30 C4
Vanguard Rd DE24. . 56 A2
Varley St DE24 . . . . 37 C2
Vauxhall Rd DE24 . . 26 C3
Ventnor Ho DE24 . . . 39 B3
Verbena Dr DE23 . . . 45 A4
Vermont Dr DE21 . . 21 B2
Vernon Dr DE21 . . . 31 B4
Vernongate DE1 . . . 18 A1
Vernon St DE1. . . . . 18 A1
Verona Way DE73 . . 47 B2
Vestry Rd DE21 . . . . 14 A3
Vetchfield Cl DE24 . 45 C2
Vicarage Ave DE23 . 27 A2
Vicarage Cl DE56 . . . 2 C2
Vicarage Ct DE21 . . 24 C1
Vicarage Dr DE21 . . 20 C3
Vicarage La
Duffield DE56 . . . . . . 7 B3
Little Eaton DE21 . . . 10 A1
Vicarage Rd
Belper DE56 . . . . 4 A2

Vicarage Rd continued
Chellaston DE73 . . . . 47 C2
Derby DE1. . . . . 24 B2
Vicarwood Ave
Derby DE22. . . . . 12 B1
Holbrook DE56 . . . . . 5 A1
Victor Ave DE22 . . . 18 B4
Victoria Ave
Borrowash DE72. . . . 32 A2
Draycott DE72 . . . . . 40 C1
Victoria Cl DE3 . . . . 25 A4
Victoria Rd DE72. . . 40 C1
Victoria St
Castle Donington
DE74 . . . . 53 B3
Derby DE1. . . . . 61 B3
Melbourne DE73. . . 59 A2
Victoria Way DE24 . 29 A3
Victory Rd DE24 . . . 37 A2
Village Cl DE56 . . . . . 7 C2
Village St DE23 . . . . 36 B4
Villa St DE72. . . . . . 41 A1
Vincent Ave DE21. . . 31 A3
Vincent Cl DE56 . . . . 6 B2
Vincent St DE23 . . . 27 B1
Vine Cl DE23. . . . . . 35 A3
Viola Cl DE21 . . . . . 15 B3
Violet St DE23 . . . . . 27 B1
Viscount Rd DE74. . . 56 C1
Vivian St DE1 . . . . . . 19 A4
Vulcan St DE23 . . . . 28 A1

W

Wade Ave DE23 . . . . 26 B2
Wadebridge Gr
DE24 . . . . 39 B1
Wade Dr DE3 . . . . . . 25 A2
Wade St DE23 . . . . . 26 B1
Wagtail Cl DE74 . . . 53 C2
Wakami Cres DE73. . 48 A3
Wakefield Cl DE74 . . 53 C2
Walbrook Rd DE23. . 27 B1
Walcote Cl DE56 . . . 3 C3
Waldene Dr DE24 . . 38 C2
Waldorf Ave DE24 . . 38 C3
Waldorf Cl DE24 . . . 38 C3
Walgrave Cl DE56. . . 3 A4
Walk Cl DE72 . . . . . . 40 C1
Walker La DE1. . . . . 60 B4
Walk The DE56. . . . . . 6 C2
Wallace St DE22 . . . 17 B1
Wallfields Cl DE65 . . 43 A2
Wallis Cl DE72 . . . . . 40 C1
Walnut Ave DE24 . . 39 A3
Walnut Cl
Aston-on-T DE72. . . . 51 B3
Chellaston DE73 . . . . 50 C4
Walnut Rd DE56 . . . . 3 A1
Walnut St DE24 . . . . 37 B3
Walpole St DE21 . . . 19 C2
Walsham Ct DE21. . . 13 C1
Walter Evans CE Prim
Sch DE22. . . . . 12 B2
Walter St
Derby DE1. . . . . 18 A3
Draycott DE72 . . . . . 40 B2
Waltham Ave DE24. . 45 C4
Walthamstow Dr
DE22 . . . . 17 A2
Walton Ave DE24 . . 47 B4
Walton Dr DE23. . . . 36 A3
Walton Hill
Castle Donington
DE74 . . . . 53 A2
Isley Walton DE74 . . 55 A1
Walton Rd DE21 . . . 20 B1
Wansfell Cl DE3 . . . . 25 A1

Wardlow Ave DE21. . 20 C4
Ward's La DE72. . . . . 41 C2
Ward St DE22 . . . . . 27 A4
Wardwick DE1. . . . . 60 B3
Warke Flatt DE74 . . 53 B4
Warner St
Derby DE22. . . . . 61 A1
Derby, Mickleover
DE3 . . . . 24 C1
Warrendale Ct
DE73 . . . . 48 A2
Warren St DE24. . . . 38 B4
Warwick Ave DE3 . . 36 C1
Warwick Gdns DE56 . 3 C1
Warwick St DE24 . . 28 C2
Washington Ave
DE21 . . . . 21 A2
Washington Cl
DE73 . . . . 59 A2
Washington Cotts
DE72. . . . . 32 C1
Waterford Dr DE21. . 30 A4
Watergo La DE23 . . 33 C3
Waterloo Ct DE1. . . 60 C5
Watermeadow Rd
DE24 . . . . 38 C1
Watermint Cl DE23 . 35 A2
Waterside Cl DE22. . 12 C3
Waterside Ho DE1 . . 60 B4
Watson St DE1. . . . . 18 A2
Watten Cl DE24. . . . 45 C2
Waveney Cl DE24 . . . 9 C1
Waverley St DE24 . . 37 C3
Wayfaring Rd DE21 . 14 C1
Wayzgoose Dr
DE21 . . . . 19 B2
Weavers Cl
Belper DE56 . . . . 3 B3
Borrowash DE72. . . . 32 C1
Weavers Gn DE3 . . . 24 B1
Webster St DE1. . . . 61 A2
Weirfield Rd DE22 . . 12 C2
Welbeck Gr DE22 . . 11 C3
Welland Cl DE3 . . . . 24 C4
Wellesley Ave DE3 . . 35 C3
Wellington Cres
DE1 . . . . 61 D2
Wellington Ct 1
DE56 . . . . 2 B1
Wellington St DE1 . . 61 D2
Well La DE56 . . . . . . 4 A1
Wells Cl DE23 . . . . . 34 A3
Wells Rd DE3 . . . . . 25 A2
Well St DE1. . . . . . . 60 B5
Well Yd
Belper DE56 . . . . 2 C3
Holbrook DE56 . . . . . 5 A1
Welney Cl DE3 . . . . 33 C4
Welshpool Rd DE21 13 C1
Welton Ave DE56 . . . 3 A4
Welwyn Ave
Derby, Alleton
DE24 . . . . 47 B4
Derby DE22. . . . . 11 C3
Wembley Gdns
DE22 . . . . 16 C2
Wendover Cl DE3 . . 24 B1
Wenlock Cl DE3 . . . 25 A1
Wensleydale Wlk
DE24 . . . . 39 B3
Wensley Dr DE21 . . 31 B3
Wentworth Cl DE3 . . 25 B2
Wentworth Ho 1
DE1 . . . . 18 A1
Werburgh Cl DE21 . . 30 C4

Werburgh St DE22 . . 61 A2
Wesley La DE72. . . . . 23 B1
Wesley Rd DE24 . . . . 39 A1
Wessington Mews
DE22 . . . . 12 A1
West Ave
Chellaston DE73. . . . 47 B3
Derby DE1. . . . . 60 A4
Draycott DE72 . . . . . 40 B2
West Bank Ave
DE22 . . . . 18 B4
West Bank Cl DE22. . 18 A4
West Bank Rd DE22 . . 8 C1
Westbourne Pk
DE22 . . . . 16 B3
Westbury Ct DE22. . . 27 A3
Westbury Gdns DE56. . 3 B3
Westbury St DE22. . . 27 A3
West Cl DE22 . . . . 12 A2
West Croft Ave
DE23 . . . . 35 C1
Westdene Ave
DE24 . . . . 37 C1
West Dr DE3. . . . . 24 C2
Western Rd
Derby DE3. . . . . 25 A2
Derby, Rose Hill
DE23 . . . . 27 C3
Westfield Derby
DE1. . . . . 61 C2
Westfield Gr DE22 . . 26 C4
Westgate DE1 . . . . . . 18 A2
West Gr DE24. . . . . . . 37 C1
Westgreen Ave
DE24 . . . . 37 C1
Westhall Rd DE3. . . . 24 C3
West Lawn DE65 . . . . 43 A2
Westleigh Ave
DE22 . . . . 17 B2
Westminster St
DE24 . . . . 38 B4
Westmorland Cl
DE21 . . . . 19 B2
Weston Park Ave
DE24 . . . . 47 B3
Weston Park Gdns
DE24 . . . . 47 A3
Weston Rd DE72. . . . 51 A4
Weston Rise DE73 . . 50 C4
West Park Rd DE22 . . 18 A4
West Park Sch
DE21 . . . . 21 C1
West Rd DE21 . . . . . . 21 C1
West Row DE22. . . . . 12 C1
West Service Rd
DE21 . . . . 30 A3
West View Ave
DE23 . . . . 35 A3
Westwood Dr DE24 . 37 C1
Wetherby Rd DE24. . 38 A3
Weyacres DE72 . . . . . 32 B1
Wharfedale Cl
DE22 . . . . 13 A4
Wheatcroft Way
DE21 . . . . 13 B2
Wheathill Gr DE23 . . 34 C2
Wheatland Cl DE24 . . 44 C2
Wheatsheaf Cl
DE21 . . . . 15 B2

Wheeldon Ave
Belper DE56 . . . . 3 A2
Derby DE22. . . . . 18 A3
Wheeldon Manor
DE22 . . . . 18 A4
Wheelwright Way
DE24 . . . . 28 C3
Whenby Cl DE3 . . . . . 24 B2
Whernside Cl DE24 . 39 C2
Whilton Ct DE56 . . . . . 3 C2
Whinbush Ave
DE24 . . . . 38 A1
Whistlestop Cl DE3 . 24 C4
Whiston St DE23 . . . . 27 C2
Whitaker Gdns
DE23 . . . . 27 A2
Whitaker Rd DE23 . . 27 A2
Whitaker St DE23 . . . 27 C2
Whitby Ave DE21 . . . 13 B1
Whitecross Gdns
DE1. . . . . 18 A3
Whitecross Ho DE1 . 18 A3
Whitecross St DE1 . . 18 A3
White Hart Yd DE56 . . 6 A2
Whitehaven Gr
DE73 . . . . 48 A3
Whitehouse Cl
DE24 . . . . 47 A3
Whitehouse Rise
DE56 . . . . 2 A4
Whitehurst St DE24 . 37 C3
WHITE MOOR. 3 B3
Whitemoor Hall
DE56 . . . . 3 C3
Whitemoor La DE56. . 3 C3
White St DE22 . . . . . 18 A3
Whiteway DE22 . . . . 12 A2
Whitewell Gdns
DE24 . . . . 39 B1
Whitmore Rd DE21 . . 20 B2
Whitstable Cl DE23 . 35 C3
Whitt Cl DE72 . . . . . . 32 B1
Whittington St
DE24 . . . . 37 C2
Whittlebury Dr
DE23 . . . . 34 B3
Whyteleafe Gr
DE21 . . . . 15 A1
Wickersley Cl 🔢
DE22 . . . . 12 B2
Wicksteed Cl DE56. . . 3 C3
Widdybank Cl DE22 . 11 B2
Wigmore Cl DE24 . . . 39 B1
Wilcock Ho DE21 . . . 19 B2
Wilders Lea Ct DE56 . 4 B4
Wildersley Rd DE56. . 4 B3
Wildsmith St DE24. . 38 C4
Wild St DE22 . . . . 17 C1
Wilfred St DE23. . . . . 28 A2
Wilkins Dr DE24 . . . . 38 A3
Willesden Ave
DE22 . . . . 16 C3
Willetts Rd DE21. . . . 20 C3
William Cl DE56 . . . . . 7 A3
William Gilbert
Endowed Prim Sch
DE56 . . . . 7 B3
William St
Belper DE56 . . . . 2 B2
Derby DE1. . . . . 18 A2
Willn St DE23 . . . . . . 27 B1

Willowbrook Grange
DE73 . . . . 48 A1
Willow Cl
Aston-on-T DE72. . . . 51 B2
Derby DE72. . . . . 12 B2
Willow Croft DE24 . . 48 C4
Willowcroft Rd
DE21 . . . . 31 A4
Willow Farm Bsns Pk
DE74 . . . . 53 B4
Willow Farm Ct
DE65 . . . . 43 A2
Willow Gr DE56. . . . . . 4 B4
Willowherb Cl
DE24 . . . . 45 C2
Willow Ho DE21 . . . . 19 B2
Willow Park Way
DE72 . . . . 51 A2
Willow Rd DE74. . . . . 53 B3
Willow Row DE1. . . . 60 A4
Willowsend Cl
DE65 . . . . 43 A1
Willowside Gn
DE21 . . . . 30 C3
Willson Ave DE23 . . . 35 C4
Willson Rd DE23 . . . . 35 B4
Wilmington Ave
DE24 . . . . 39 A1
Wilmore Rd DE24. . . 37 A1
WILMORTON. 29 A2
Wilmot Ave DE21 . . . 20 B1
Wilmot Rd DE56 . . . . . 2 C2
Wilmot St DE1. . . . . . 61 B2
Wilmslow Dr DE21. . 15 A1
Wilson Cl DE3 . . . . . . 33 B4
Wilson Rd DE21. . . . . 20 B4
Wilson St DE1 . . . . . . 61 B2
Wilsthorpe Rd
DE21 . . . . 20 C3
Wilton Cl DE24 . . . . . 44 C2
Wiltra Gr DE56. . . . . . . 7 C2
Wiltshire Rd DE21 . . 20 A3
Wimbledon Rd
DE22 . . . . 16 C3
Wimbourne Cl
DE73 . . . . 48 A2
Wimpole Gdns
DE22 . . . . 17 A2
Wincanton Cl DE24 . 28 C1
Winchcombe Way
DE21 . . . . 15 A2
Windermere Cres
DE22 . . . . 12 A3
Windermere Dr
DE21 . . . . 22 A1
Windley Cres DE22. . 12 B1
Windmill Ave DE56. . . 6 B2
Windmill Cl
Castle Donington
DE74 . . . . 56 B4
Elvaston DE24. . . . . . 49 A4
Ockbrook DE72. . . . . 23 B1
Windmill Hill La
DE22 . . . . 17 B2
Windmill La DE56. . . . 2 C2
Windmill Rd DE65 . . 58 A3
Windmill Rise DE56. . 2 C3
Windrush Cl DE21 . . . 9 C1
Windsor Ave
Derby DE23. . . . . 35 A4
Melbourne DE73. . . . 59 A3
Windsor Cl DE72. . . . 32 B1

Windsor Ct DE3 . . . . . 24 C3
Windsor Dr DE21 . . . 22 C2
Wingerworth Park Rd
DE22 . . . . 22 A1
Wingfield Dr DE21 . . 14 C3
Winslow Gn DE21 . . . 21 B2
Winster Cl DE56 . . . . . 3 A3
Winster Rd DE21. . . . 14 A1
Wintergreen Dr
DE23 . . . . 34 B2
Wisgreaves Rd
DE24 . . . . 38 B4
Witham Dr DE3. . . . . 23 C4
Witney Cl DE24 . . . . . 37 B4
Witton Ct DE24 . . . . . 45 A4
Woburn Pl DE22 . . . . 17 A1
Wolfa St DE22 . . . . . . 61 A2
Wollaton Rd DE21 . . 20 B4
Wollaton Rd N 🔢
DE21 . . . . 14 B1
Wolverley Grange
DE24 . . . . 39 C2
Woodale Cl DE23 . . . 34 B2
Woodbeck Ct DE21 . 15 A2
Woodbridge Cl
DE73 . . . . 47 C1
Woodchester Dr
DE24 . . . . 39 C2
Woodcock Sq DE3 . . 33 B4
Woodcote Way
DE23 . . . . 34 C3
Wood Croft DE23 . . . 35 C4
Woodford Rd DE22. . 16 C3
Woodgate Dr DE73 . 48 A1
Woodhall Dr DE23 . . 34 A4
Woodhouse Rd DE56,
DE7 . . . . 6 B1
Woodhurst Cl DE21 . 19 C4
Wood La DE56 . . . . 4 A1
Woodland Ave
DE72 . . . . 32 B2
Woodland Rd DE22 . 18 A4
Woodlands Ave
DE24 . . . . 47 B4
Woodlands Cl
Little Eaton DE21 . . . . 9 C4
Melbourne DE73. . . . 59 A3
Woodlands Com Sch
DE22 . . . . 11 C4
Woodlands La
Chellaston DE73. . . . 50 C4
Quarndon DE22 . . . . . 8 B2
Woodlands Rd DE22 . 8 C1
Woodlands The
DE73 . . . . 59 B3
Woodlands Way
DE73 . . . . 59 B3
Woodlands Yd
DE73 . . . . 50 C4
Woodlea Gr DE21 . . . 10 A4
Woodminton Dr
DE73 . . . . 47 C3
Wood Rd
Derby, Chaddesden
DE21 . . . . 20 C4
Derby, Oakwood
DE21 . . . . 14 B1
Derby, Spondon
DE21 . . . . 22 C2
Woodrising Cl
DE21 . . . . 15 A3

Woodroffe Wlk
DE23 . . . . 36 A3
Woodside Dr DE22. . 12 C4
Woods La DE22 . . . . . 61 A1
Woods Mdw DE72 . . 39 C1
Woodsorrel Dr
DE21 . . . . 15 A3
Wood St DE1 . . . . 60 C4
Woodstock Cl DE22 . 11 C4
Woodthorne Ave
DE24 . . . . 47 B4
Woodthorpe Ave
DE21 . . . . 20 B2
Woodview Gdns
DE22 . . . . 18 B4
Woodwards Cl
DE72 . . . . 32 C1
Woolrych St DE23 . . 27 B2
Worcester Cres
DE21 . . . . 20 A4
Wordsworth Ave
DE24 . . . . 36 B1
Wordsworth Dr
DE24 . . . . 36 C1
Wragley Way DE24. . 45 A2
Wren Park Cl
Belper DE56 . . . . 2 A3
Findern DE65 . . . . . . 43 A1
Wren Park Prim Sch
DE3. . . . . 25 C2
Wren Way DE3. . . . . . 33 A3
Wretham Cl DE3. . . . 33 C4
Wroxham Cl DE24. . . 47 A4
Wyaston Cl DE22 . . . 12 A1
Wye St DE24 . . . . 38 C4
Wyndham St DE24 . . 38 C3
Wynton Ave DE24 . . 38 B4
Wyver La DE56. . . . . . . 2 B4
Wyvern Bsns Pk
DE21 . . . . 29 C2
Wyvernside DE21 . . . 29 B4
Wyvern Way DE21 . . 29 C4

Y

Yardley Way DE56. . . . 3 C2
Yarmouth Ho DE24 . 39 B3
Yarrow Cl DE24 . . . . . 45 B2
Yarwell Cl DE21 . . . . 13 C1
Yates Ave DE72 . . . . . 51 A2
Yates St DE23. . . . . . 27 C1
Yeovil Cl DE24 . . . . . . 39 B3
Yewdale Gr DE21 . . . 15 B3
Yews Cl DE73 . . . . 48 A1
Yew Tree Ave DE72 . 23 C1
Yew Tree Cl DE24 . . . 39 B3
Yew Tree La DE72 . . 49 C4
York Rd DE21 . . . . . . 20 B3
York St DE1 . . . . 18 A1
Youlgreave Cl DE21. 14 B1
Young St DE23 . . . . . 27 B1
Yoxall Dr DE22. . . . . 26 B4
Ypres Rd DE22 . . . . . 11 B2

Z

Zetland Cres DE24 . . 44 C2

List of numbered locations

In some busy areas of the maps it is not always possible to show the name of every place.

Where not all names will fit, some smaller places are shown by a number. If you wish to find out the name associated with a number, use this listing.

The places in this list are also listed normally in the Index.

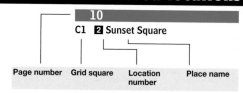

Page number   Grid square   Location number   Place name

2	
B1	**1** Wellington Ct
	2 Cheapside
	3 Belle Acre Cl
	4 Heritage Ct
	5 Brook Cl
	6 Leighton Way
	7 Midland View
B2	**1** St George's Pl
	2 Crown Terr
	3 Clusters Ct
	4 Short Row
	5 Field Row
	10 St Laurence Gdns
	11 Bridgefield Ct

11	
C2	**1** Carsington Ho
	2 Norbury Ct
	3 Kedleston Ct

12	
B2	**1** Wickersley Cl
	2 Maltby Cl
	4 St Matthew's Wlk
B3	**1** Birchover Ho
	2 Church La N
	3 Tudor Ct

13	
C1	**1** Kendal Wlk
	2 Ledbury Pl
	3 Malvern Way
	4 Filey Wlk
	5 Seascale Cl
	6 Redcar Gdns

14	
B1	**1** Ingledew Cl
	2 Heathermead Cl
	3 Beamwood Cl
	4 Tansley Rise
	5 Wollaton Rd N
B2	**1** Cardinal Cl
	2 Sedgebrook Cl
	3 Somerby Way
	4 Garthorpe Ct
	5 Tweeds Muir Cl
	6 Pykestone Cl
	7 Houghton Ct
	8 Rutherford Rise
	9 Paddock Croft

18	
A1	**1** Wentworth Ho
	2 Alexandra Mills
	3 Rowleys Mill

	4 Langton The
B3	**1** King's Mead Ho
	2 Strutt's Park Ho
	3 Belper Rd
	4 Milford St

20	
A4	**1** Ashover Rd
	2 Taddington Cl
	3 Ringwood Cl
	4 Liverpool St

24	
C1	**1** Morley Ho
	2 Bramble Mews
	3 Limes Ct
	4 Parade The
	5 Meadow Ct
	6 All Saints Ct

27	
C2	**1** Peterhouse Terr
	3 Industrial St
	4 Provident St

28	
A2	**1** Arthur Ct
	2 Tintagel Cl
	3 Alexandra Gdns

39	
B2	**1** Stonesdale Ct
	2 Swaledale Ct
	3 Airedale Wlk
	4 Arkendale Wlk
	5 Farndale Ct
	6 Compton Cl

45	
A3	**1** Craiglee Ct
	2 Edgelaw Ct
	3 Mull Ct
	4 Lindisfarne Cl
	5 Blackmount Ct
	6 Lismore Ct
	7 Dalness Ct
	8 Campsie Ct
	9 Stornoway Cl
	10 Shandwick Ct
	11 Braemar Cl
	12 Kirkland Way
	13 Padstow Cl
	14 Tavistock Cl

59	
A3	**1** Loake Ct
	2 Croft The
	3 Redway Croft
	4 Lampad Cl

60	
A4	**1** Abels Mill
	2 Middle Mill
	3 Brook Ho
	4 Longs Mill

61	
B2	**1** Hillview Ho
	2 Davis Ho
	3 Swinscoe Ho
	4 Sterndale Ho
	5 Eldon Ho

PHILIP'S MAPS
the Gold Standard for drivers

◆ **Philip's street atlases cover every county in England, Wales, Northern Ireland and much of Scotland**

◆ Every named street is shown, including alleys, lanes and walkways

◆ Thousands of additional features marked: stations, public buildings, car parks, places of interest

◆ Route-planning maps to get you close to your destination

◆ Postcodes on the maps and in the index

◆ Widely used by the emergency services, transport companies and local authorities

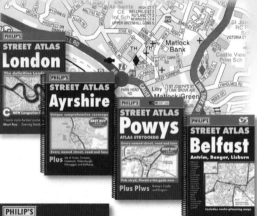

For national mapping, choose
Philip's Navigator Britain
the most detailed road atlas available of England, Wales and Scotland. Hailed by Auto Express as 'the ultimate road atlas', the atlas shows every road and lane in Britain.

'The ultimate in UK mapping'
The Sunday Times

Street atlases currently available

England
Bedfordshire
Berkshire
Birmingham and West Midlands
Bristol and Bath
Buckinghamshire
Cambridgeshire
Cheshire
Cornwall
Cumbria
Derbyshire
Devon
Dorset
County Durham and Teesside
Essex
North Essex
South Essex
Gloucestershire
Hampshire
North Hampshire
South Hampshire
Herefordshire Monmouthshire
Hertfordshire
Isle of Wight
Kent
East Kent
West Kent
Lancashire
Leicestershire and Rutland
Lincolnshire
London
Greater Manchester
Merseyside
Norfolk
Northamptonshire
Northumberland
Nottinghamshire
Oxfordshire
Shropshire
Somerset
Staffordshire
Suffolk
Surrey

East Sussex
West Sussex
Tyne and Wear
Warwickshire
Birmingham and West Midlands
Wiltshire and Swindon
Worcestershire
East Yorkshire Northern Lincolnshire
North Yorkshire
South Yorkshire
West Yorkshire

Wales
Anglesey, Conwy and Gwynedd
Cardiff, Swansea and The Valleys
Carmarthenshire, Pembrokeshire and Swansea
Ceredigion and South Gwynedd
Denbighshire, Flintshire, Wrexham
Herefordshire Monmouthshire
Powys

Scotland
Aberdeenshire
Ayrshire
Dumfries and Galloway
Edinburgh and East Central Scotland
Fife and Tayside
Glasgow and West Central Scotland
Inverness and Moray
Lanarkshire
Scottish Borders

Northern Ireland
County Antrim and County Londonderry
County Armagh and County Down
Belfast
County Tyrone and County Fermanagh

How to order
Philip's maps and atlases are available from bookshops, motorway services and petrol stations. You can order direct from the publisher by phoning **0207 531 8473** or online at **www.philips-maps.co.uk**
For bulk orders only, e-mail philips@philips-maps.co.uk